Overcoming the Evil One

Dr. Jason Pfledderer

© 2023 JASON PFLEDDERER. All rights reserved.

ISBN: 9798388837639

All rights reserved. No part of this book may be reproduced or transmitted in any form or by any means, mechanical or electronic, including photocopying or recording or by any information storage and retrieval system, or transmitted by email without permission except with brief quotations embodied in critical reviews or articles.

All quotations in this book are from the ESV translation unless otherwise noted.

The ESV® Bible (The Holy Bible, English Standard Version®). ESV® Text Edition: 2016. Copyright © 2001 by Crossway, a publishing ministry of Good News Publishers.

The King James Version. The KJV is public domain in the United States.

New American Standard Bible®, Copyright © 1960, 1971, 1977, 1995, 2020 by The Lockman Foundation. All rights reserved.

Cover design by: K&T Graphics

Edited by: Eve Editing Services

Disclaimer

A cardinal rule of biblical interpretation of any written document is always **"context rules."** My job as a biblical expositor is always to determine the meaning that the original biblical author — and ultimately God Himself — intended a passage to mean. Therefore, I use the acronym S.T.O.P as a guideline for biblical interpretation:

Situation — What is the situation in this passage? Read the passage for context. What is the specific <u>situation</u> in this passage?

Type of literature — Is this passage poetry, narrative, prophetic, or apocalyptic? Different literature has different rules of interpretation. Poetry and prophetic writing, for example, contain many figures of speech that are not to be interpreted literally but figuratively. Isaiah 13 is a good example:

> *Behold, the day of the Lord comes, cruel, with wrath and fierce anger, to make the land desolation and to destroy its sinners from it. For the stars of the heavens and their constellations will not give their light; the sun will be dark at its rising, and the moon will not shed its light.*

This is prophetic hyperbole. God often uses cosmic deconstruction language in passages foretelling judgment upon a nation, as in this passage prophesying judgment on Babylon. The same language occurs again later when God foretold judgment upon Egypt. Jesus used the same imagery in Matthew's Gospel when he described the impending judgment on the covenant people of Israel that was fulfilled in the destruction of Jerusalem in 70 AD. Failure to appreciate such phenomena of language has led to all kinds of heresy and even the establishment of many religious cults.

Object of the passage — What is the object of this passage? What is the point the author is making? Again, context must determine what the <u>object</u> of the passage is.

Prescriptive or descriptive — Not every passage is prescriptive. Much biblical narrative is telling a story of what happened in a particular instance, and there is no indication in the text that a general prescription is being made. A good example is the story of Elijah dousing the wood. He was a prophet of God, and his story is not a model of what every New Testament Christian should do today!

I give you this guide to help you consider Scripture and not to ignore context. Context is always the key in biblical interpretation; otherwise, an individual is using God's word unethically and can make it mean just about anything they desire. Therefore, I would like to make this disclaimer:

With the vast array of denominations and the large numbers of theologians, there is a myriad of opinions on biblical topics. Knowing this, I have tried to align the contents of this book as closely as possible with Scripture. I hope you enjoy it!

Acknowledgements

God has blessed me beyond reason throughout my life. Not only has He given me the Holy Spirit who aims me in the right direction, but also surrounds me with the most perfect examples of intelligence, wisdom, and strength. I give all the glory to God first and those who lead me to His understanding second.

My leadership is not something I can boast about. God and His people have bestowed upon me much knowledge. The reason I can see so far is not only due to my vision, but also from the great teachers, friends, mentors, and colleagues whose shoulders I have stood upon throughout my life. After years of being led by them, I am now sharing this information with you.

I'd like to thank the Holy Spirit first for even speaking to me and to God the Father for sending His Son Jesus Christ to pay the penalty for my sins and not giving me the punishment that I so rightfully deserve.

I would like to specifically thank Pastor Mark Kline for his study notes (which were used with permission); Professor Roger Krynock, who keeps me theologically correct; Emma, who makes sure it all "flows" without a hitch; and finally, Natasha, who puts my vision into picture form. Without all of you, this and many other projects wouldn't have been possible. May God bless you all.

Table of Contents

Chapter 1: Our Enemy 1
Chapter 2: Three Things 7
Chapter 3: A Plan 9
Chapter 4: No Blurred Lines 13
Chapter 5: Creation 17
Chapter 6: Origin of the Evil One 21
Chapter 7: Free Will 27
Chapter 8: Focus 29
Chapter 9: Rejoice 33
Chapter 10: The Names of the Evil One 35
Chapter 11: The Devil's Names 37
Chapter 12: God of This World 41
Chapter 13: Pride 45
Chapter 14: A Tempter 49
Chapter 15: A Thief 51
Chapter 16: Angel of Light 53
Chapter 17: Biblical Influence 57
Chapter 18: Definitions 59
Chapter 20: Of the World 65
Chapter 22: Order 69
Chapter 23: Control 73
Chapter 24: Believe God's Word 79

Chapter 25: God's Power 81

Chapter 26: Three Things 83

Chapter 27: The Battleground 85

Chapter 28: The Devil's Methods 91

Chapter 29: God Can Deliver 99

Chapter 30: Dominated 103

Chapter 31: Two Dangers 107

Chapter 32: The Enemy's Abilities 111

Chapter 33: More about the Enemy's Tactics 115

Chapter 34: Fight Him 119

Chapter 35: The Calling 123

Chapter 36: Jesus Came 127

Chapter 37: How Jesus Dealt with the Evil One 131

Chapter 38: Jesus' Tactics 135

Chapter 39: Jesus' Teachings 137

Chapter 40: His Kingdom 141

Chapter 41: Power, Right, and Authority 143

Chapter 41: Christ Has Power 147

Chapter 42: God Gave Us His Name 153

Chapter 43: Power to Witness 157

Chapter 44: The Unbeliever 159

Chapter 45: The Whole Armor of God 163

Chapter 46: Six Parts 165

Chapter 47: Truth 167
Chapter 48: Righteousness 169
Chapter 49: Peace 171
Chapter 50: Faith 173
Chapter 51: Salvation 175
Chapter 52: God's Word 177
Chapter 53: The Ultimate End—Victory of the Saints 179
Chapter 54: The Times 183
Chapter 55: Rapture 189
Chapter 56: Judgment of the Enemy 193
Chapter 57: Hear the Word of God and Do It 195
Salvation Prayer 197

CHAPTER 1

Our Enemy

After this manner, therefore, pray ye: Our Father which art in heaven, Hallowed be thy name. Thy kingdom come, Thy will be done in earth, as it is in heaven. Give us this day our daily bread. And forgive us our debts, as we forgive our debtors. And lead us not into temptation, but deliver us from evil: For thine is the kingdom, and the power, and the glory, for ever. Amen. (Matthew 6:9-13, KJV)

Jesus gave this prayer as a way to teach His followers how we ought to pray.

Jesus tells us to pray: *deliver us from the evil one.*

Jesus taught that believers should pray for deliverance from the temptations of the devil.

The word "deliver" means "rescue". The word "deliver" that Jesus used means to cause someone in peril to be delivered or to escape real danger.

This world we live in is full of all kinds of evil—filth and degradation, child abuse, spousal abuse, sexual abuse, and domestic violence. Abortion takes the lives of 1.3 million babies per year; that's 43 million children since 1973!

OUR ENEMY

Pornography is an $18 billion a year business. 21,570 murders were committed in the United States in 2021.[1] Drug use is at an all-time high. Divorce (which by the way has gone down in the last few years) is still high, occurring in over 43% of marriages.

Adultery is committed as a regular way of living. Rebellion against families committed by children is a terrible thing that is not going away. Petty theft is a huge problem in our country. Do you ever open up the local paper and look at the list of things that have been destroyed or stolen over the course of 24 hours in your community or throughout the nation?

At this point, it's easy to say without any doubt that we live in a dark and evil world.

But what is the source of that evil? Could it be that there is a grand design of destruction?

The Bible has much to say on this issue, my friend. And it points to one source, one power behind all the evil that is in the world. And that one source, that one power is the evil one, Satan, the devil, our adversary, and the opponent of Almighty God.

This movement towards evil and the devil is characteristic of the time in which we live. The Bible says the latter days will bring a departure from the faith. Every sign that we see points to the fact that we are in the latter days; we are in the end times. We are so close to seeing Christ return to

---

[1] https://www.cnn.com/2021/10/06/health/us-homicide-rate-increase-nchs-study/index.html. Retrieved 6/6/2022.

split the skies, and we will see Him, and our world will be caught as a thief in the night. It will be too late then for sinners to repent.

Our culture is becoming more and more pagan. Consider the progression of entertainment, for example, from what was seemingly innocent in the 50s, to the plainly demonic entertainment that is given to us today. With that, we often see a progression from occasional viewing, where people would watch a movie once in a while or watch the TV once in a while, to a lifestyle of binging this type of content. Did you know that many people now live their lives solely to be entertained?

Nowadays, we can get entertainment from our phones, computers, and tablets, as well as pretty much any store you can imagine. People seek entertainment at casinos, race tracks, and football stadiums, to name a few. We as human beings feel that we now deserve to be constantly entertained. All we do is take in mindless drivel and demonic influence that is disguised as mindless entertainment. The whole of society is moving towards evil.

Now the Spirit speaketh expressly, that in the latter days, some will depart from the faith, giving heed to deceiving spirits, and doctrines of demons. (Timothy 4:1, KJV)

Look at the end of that Scripture. Some will depart from the faith, belief in Christ, and give heed to deceiving spirits, and seducing spirits. Now, these are very subtle spirits. They will seduce you, draw you away from faith in Christ and pull you into the doctrines of demons. Did you know that the devil has doctrines? The devil has doctrines. One of them is

OUR ENEMY

that homosexuality is okay. One of them is that Jesus is not God. Another is that the blood of Jesus Christ cannot cleanse you from your sin.

> ***Not only is there a movement towards evil in this time in which we live, but there is a spiritual battle that is being fought for the hearts and minds of men and women, boys and girls.***

Look to Ephesians chapter 6 verse 10-12:

Finally, be strong in the Lord and in the strength of his might. Put on the whole armor of God, that you may be able to stand against the schemes of the devil. For we do not wrestle against flesh and blood, but against the rulers, against the authorities, against the cosmic powers over this present darkness, against the spiritual forces of evil in the heavenly places.

We do not wrestle against flesh and blood. In the original Greek language, the word translated "wrestle" is "palē," and it refers to the struggle between the saints and the spirit rebels who are against God. We do not wrestle against flesh and blood, but against spiritual hosts of wickedness in high places; spiritual hosts that have plans and purposes against you, against me, and the people of this world.

The Bible says that Satan is the prince, the power of the air; he is the "god" of this world. Satan is a prince that stands at the top of the ranks of the demons, the hosts of spiritual wickedness in high places, and he sends them out to do his bidding. He sends them out to carry out his schemes and plans against you, and your family, and the church and this society, and he fully intends and plans on taking as many people to hell, the lake of fire with him as he possibly can.

Satin hates you and his designs against you and your family are for your destruction.

We are fighting against an organized enemy that is incredibly intelligent and wise in the ways of war. If you think you can fight the evil one alone, you are sadly mistaken. The only possible way that we can defeat this enemy is through the power of the Holy Spirit and having a solid knowledge of the word of God.

You cannot even begin to fathom the plans that the devil has against the church, you, and your family. He will deceive you by seeking to influence you toward making decisions that are against the will of God. The only possible way we'll be able to stand against this enemy is by knowing the truth of God's word and being filled with the Holy Spirit.

CHAPTER 2

Three Things

Finally, be strong in the Lord and in the strength of his might. Put on the whole armor of God, that you may be able to stand against the schemes of the devil. For we do not wrestle against flesh and blood, but against the rulers, against the authorities, against the cosmic powers over this present darkness, against the spiritual forces of evil in the heavenly places. (Ephesians 6:10-12)

In this Scripture, I see three things that we must be aware of. First, I see that this is an organized enemy – an enemy with ranks, rulers, workers, principalities, powers, and spiritual hosts of wickedness in high places. Secondly, I see that the enemy has fully pitted himself against us. Jesus tells us that He has come that we may have life and that we may have it more abundantly. Now thirdly, there is a Creator God in control of His creation.

These are the three things that I base all this teaching concerning "the evil one" on.

1. There is an increasing rebellion against God and a yielding to the influence of the devil in the days that we live.

2. There is a spiritual battle going on that we are a part of one way or another.

3. The most important one of all is that there is a Creator God that is in control of His creation. Colossians 1:15-16 says:

THREE THINGS

> *He is the image of the invisible God, the firstborn of all creation. For by him all things were created, in heaven and on earth, visible and invisible, whether thrones or dominions or rulers or authorities—all things were created through him and for him. (Colossians 1:15-16)*

Even the devil was created by God. Read that again. Thrones, dominions, rulers, and authorities were created by God and for God.

In the next few chapters, we'll see exactly how Satan was created and how he became what he is now. This same God who created Satan is also the God that is in control of the ultimate destiny of this creation. His plan is being worked out. It is up to you and me and other believers in Christ not to remain ignorant of the devil's devices, not to be ignorant of the plan of God, but to become informed through the word of God and become obedient to God's plan.

CHAPTER 3

A Plan

God has a plan for the redemption of mankind. In 1 John 3:8, we learn that he who sins is of the devil now:

Whoever makes a practice of sinning is of the devil, for the devil has been sinning from the beginning. The reason the Son of God appeared was to destroy the works of the devil.
(1 John 3:8)

God has a plan. That plan is to destroy the works of the devil. Not only this, however; God has a plan for the redemption of the entire creation.

Revelation 22:3 says, "there shall be no more curse." This curse has been upon mankind since Genesis chapter 3. The promise of deliverance came at the same time. The Bible says in Isaiah 11:6 that:

The wolf shall dwell with the lamb, and the leopard shall lie down with the young goat, and the calf and the lion and the fattened calf together; and a little child shall lead them.

Now there are three powers or wills in the world:

1. **God**
2. **The flesh**
3. **The devil**

God is the loving one. He's good. He is the creative power. He is the holy one of these forces. God is the creative, loving, good, and holy One.

A PLAN

The devil is the hateful, evil, destructive and unholy force in the creation.

Man as he comes into the world is born with a sinful nature. We make decisions to oppose the will of God and become sinners both by nature and by choice.

That means that our default position is to be rebels against God. Like Satan, we are opposed to the God who made us.

You either serve God or you serve the devil. If you choose not to serve God, you choose to serve the devil.

It can be a hard pill to swallow for some, but that's the truth.

The Bible clearly teaches that all people are corrupted by Adam's sin through natural birth. When Adam sinned, his condemnation was imputed to all humanity—we all enter the world guilty before God.

Therefore, just as sin came into the world through one man, and death through sin, and so death spread to all men because all sinned...
(Romans 5:12)

Therefore, we come into the world as children of wrath, liable to the punishment for having a sinful nature—death.

In Romans 3:10-12 the Apostle Paul explained the rebellion of all humanity:

None is righteous, no, not one; no one understands; no one seeks for God. All have

A PLAN

turned aside; together they have become worthless; no one does good, not even one.

We enter this world with a fallen nature, and we are, therefore, without hope apart from the saving grace of God in the gospel.

CHAPTER 4

No Blurred Lines

Next, we will expose the enemy's tactics and vulnerabilities. When these biblical truths are accepted, you will be more successful in resisting the influence of the enemy.

If you have a biblical worldview, then you know that we cannot live our lives well without God's help; we have to know God's truth and live by it. But when we accept the world's view, we begin to think along the lines of the lies that are promoted through the media, printed material, and secular entertainment that we consume hour by hour by hour throughout the week.

When we accept the world's view, we find no time for the truth of the word of God in our lives. When people have a mindset of "I don't have time to read the Bible, but I watch eight hours of movies a week and 16 hours of TV," for whom do you think they're working?

The removal of the devil's subtle influence in our lives will be assured when we educate ourselves on the truths concerning the way that God says the Christian should live his life.

> ***The best way to avoid following the devil's influence is to know the truth of how we should live.***

The only way to have freedom is through Jesus Christ. The Bible tells us that we are slaves of sin without from the forgiveness of God and the change that He brings about in the lives of those He redeems.

NO BLURRED LINES

Perhaps you do not think that you need Christ because you think that you are basically a good person. God is holy, however, and He demands holiness from us.

Have you ever stolen anything? If so, you are a thief, and God's law says that we are not to steal. Have you ever used God's name in vain? If so, you have broken God's law which says that we should not use His holy name in vain. In the Old Testament, doing that was punishable by death! Have you ever looked at another person with lust? If so, Jesus said that you have already committed adultery in your heart. If you have only committed these sins—and there are so many others you have probably committed as well—you will stand guilty before the bar of God on judgment day. You need a Savior to forgive your sins and give you eternal life.

If you do not know Him today, you should also know the good news that God loves you.

For God so loved the world, that he gave his only Son, that whoever believes in him should not perish but have eternal life. (John 3:16)

God gave His Son to die on the cross so that you would not perish; His desire is that you would turn from your sin and trust in Jesus Christ as your Savior.

So how does an individual do that?

First, let me explain that it is not a "process", as many false teachers claim.

Jesus answered them:

Jesus answered them, "Truly, truly, I say to you, everyone who practices sin is a slave to sin. The slave does not remain in the house forever; the son remains forever. So if the Son sets you free, you will be free indeed." (John 8:34-36)

Look at what Paul said in Romans 4:5:

And to the one who does not work but believes in him who justifies the ungodly, his faith is counted as righteousness... (Romans 4:5)

When the Son sets a person free, it is an act of regeneration that is done by the Holy Spirit in response to faith.

The Holy Spirit's act of regeneration is not a "process."

Rather than a process, turning to Christ is an action; you must genuinely repent of your sin and have faith in the atoning work in Jesus Christ.

And they said, "Believe in the Lord Jesus, and you will be saved, you and your household. (Acts 16:31)

The times of ignorance God overlooked, but now he commands all people everywhere to repent, because he has fixed a day on which he will judge the world in righteousness by a man whom he has appointed; and of this he has given assurance to all by raising him from the dead. (Acts 17:30-31)

Now, of course you should know that God loves you and wants to save you. However, most people are very complacent about hearing this, thinking something along the lines of: "God loves me, great!"

NO BLURRED LINES

However, you need to follow God's law as well. No one responds to the gospel until he sees his need of a Savior, and that is the function of the law. Most people think that they are good enough for God to accept them just as they are. They need to be confronted with the law so that they come to realize that they are sinners who have offended God and are deserving of condemnation.

Being a Christian isn't about being perfect either; it is about devoting yourself to Christ. Now, am I perfect? Nope. Do I sin? Yep. Am I forgiven? Of course, but only through Jesus Christ.

Being a Christian isn't about being perfect, but it is about fighting against the flesh to imitate Christ, and fighting against the world in the name of Christ.

You need to rise as a warrior for God against the enemy.

God is calling people to know their power against the devil. We will rise and see people delivered and saved from the power of the enemy through those believers who know their authority in Jesus Christ. It will be your choice from here as to whether you will serve God or serve the devil. Many people call themselves Christians, but their conduct reveals something different.

CHAPTER 5

Creation

We are now going to start digging into the origins of our enemy.

I wrote this book because I see people getting whipped by the enemy every day. I don't think that people are getting beaten about by the enemy because they want to be, but because they don't know how not to be. There is a spiritual battle that is going on for the hearts and souls of mankind. The one we are fighting is the same one who is behind all of the evil that is taking place in our world: the evil one, Satan, the enemy of our souls.

***Whatever you want to call him,
there is one source of evil in this world.***

There is good and there is evil; there is right and there is wrong. There is God, and there is the devil. Through the revelation of the word of God, we see what is evil and what is good, what is right, and what is wrong. When we get the biblical viewpoint on what is going on around us, life becomes less confusing, and our direction in life becomes more sure.

Now, let's dig into the origins and fall of the evil one. First, as we established, God is the Creator. In John 1:3, the Bible says:

*All things were made through him, and without
him was not any thing made that was made.*

In Colossians 1:15-16, Scripture says:

CREATION

He is the image of the invisible God, the firstborn of all creation. For by him all things were created, in heaven and on earth, visible and invisible, whether thrones or dominions or rulers or authorities—all things were created through him and for him.

All things were created through Him and for Him.

Man did not evolve out of the slime that existed on the bottom of the ocean floor. He was created. When God created, He created only good things. The Bible says this in Genesis 1:10 when it records the creation in the six days:

God called the dry land Earth, and the waters that were gathered together he called Seas. And God saw that it was good.

The earth brought forth vegetation, plants yielding seed according to their own kinds, and trees bearing fruit in which is their seed, each according to its kind. And God saw that it was good. (Genesis 1:12)

And God set them in the firmament of the heaven to give light upon the earth, And to rule over the day and over the night, and to divide the light from the darkness: and God saw that it was good. (Genesis 1:17-18, KJV)

And God created great whales, and every living creature that moveth, which the waters brought forth abundantly, after their kind, and every

CREATION

winged fowl after his kind: and God saw that it was good. (Genesis 1:21, KJV)

And God made the beast of the earth after his kind, and cattle after their kind, and every thing that creepeth upon the earth after his kind: and God saw that it was good. (Genesis 1:25, KJV)

So God created man in his own image, in the image of God created he him; male and female created he them... And God saw every thing that he had made, and, behold, it was very good. And the evening and the morning were the sixth day. (Genesis 1:27, 31, KJV)

CHAPTER 6

Origin of the Evil One

When God creates things, one thing is certain and the Scripture is clear—God creates only good things.

God created the angels, including Satan, during creation week. Because the angels "shouted for joy" in response to God's creative work when He laid the foundations of the earth according to Job 38:4-7, we know that they were created before day four of creation week.

We know that Satan was created good, because God declared this at the end of creation week:

> *And God saw every thing that he had made,*
> *and, behold, it was very good. And the evening*
> *and the morning were the sixth day.*
> *(Genesis 1:31, KJV)*

Satan was created as an angel to serve and honor God. The New Testament records that there was a time when some of the angels rebelled against God and fell into wickedness:

> *For if God did not spare angels when they*
> *sinned, but cast them into hell and committed*
> *them to chains of gloomy darkness to be kept*
> *until the judgment... (2 Peter 2:4)*

> *And the angels who did not stay within their*
> *own position of authority, but left their proper*
> *dwelling, he has kept in eternal chains under*
> *gloomy darkness until the judgment of the great*
> *day... (Jude 1:6)*

ORIGIN OF THE EVIL ONE

According to Scripture, there was once an angelic insurrection against heaven's King.

No one tempted Satan into sin; his rebellion against God came from his own decision. It's not surprising, then, that Jesus called him "the father of lies" and "a murderer from the beginning", phrases that describe Satan from the beginning of his existence (John 8:44).

But God created Lucifer to originally be good. Ezekiel 28:11-15 give us a clearer picture of what Satan was like when God created him:

> *Moreover, the word of the Lord came to me saying, Son of man, take up a lamentation for the king of Tyrus and say to him, Thus says the Lord God, you were the seal of perfection, full of wisdom and perfect in beauty. You were in Eden, the garden of God, every precious stone was your covering, the Stardust, the topaz, the diamond, the beryl, the onyx and Jasper, Sapphire and turquoise and emerald with gold, the workmanship of your tabrets and your pipes was prepared for you on the day you were created. You were the anointed cherub who covers I established you, you were on the Holy Mountain of God, you walked back and forth in the midst of the fiery stones, you were perfect in your ways, from the day you were created.*
> *(KJV)*

Now, you see right in the beginning, it says, "the king of Tyrus". I want to raise to your attention the law of the hermeneutical principle of double reference. In this law, two things or persons are addressed in the same passage. First, there is a visible person, someone who is directly addressed. In this passage, the visible person would be the king of Tyrus. At the same time, there is an invisible person who is also addressed. So in this passage, Ezekiel is addressing the king of Tyrus, but he is also addressing the evil that is behind the king of Tyrus, and that is the evil one: Satan, who is Lucifer.

The king of Tyrus, according to Josephus, had such pride that he even claimed to be God.

And that is what the Bible taught as well:

Because your heart is proud, and you have said, 'I am a god, I sit in the seat of the gods, in the heart of the seas,' yet you are but a man, and no god, though you make your heart like the heart of a god... (Ezekiel 28:2)

Not only did he claim to be a god, but he exalted himself as the heart of God. This king claimed that what he wanted was God's will. Behind this man was evil, that one singular source of evil: Satan.

Now, in Ezekiel 28:12b, we begin to see exactly what Satan was like when God created him:

You were the signet of perfection, full of wisdom and perfect in beauty.

In the King James Version, it says:

Thou sealest up the sum.

The word "sum" means pattern. God said, "he sealed up the pattern". Think about it this way; he was the pinnacle of the pattern of creation, he was created perfectly.

ORIGIN OF THE EVIL ONE

He could have been a model of perfection of the creative power of Almighty God. He sealed up the seal of perfection and was full of wisdom.

That means he was highly intelligent, created with a mind that could think for itself that could deduce the deeper things of creation. This is how the devil was created.

In this we see that it could not be completely referencing the king of Tyrus, as no man is perfect. But Satan was created perfect in beauty; that is, he had no flaw in his beauty.

He was the seal of perfection in God's creative power.

Now in verse 13, we see that it says:

You were in Eden, the garden of God.

So, we see that Satan was present in the time of creation that we read about in the book of Genesis. He was also covered in precious stones.

Thou hast been in Eden the garden of God; every precious stone was thy covering, the sardius, topaz, and the diamond, the beryl, the onyx, and the jasper, the sapphire, the emerald, and the carbuncle, and gold: the workmanship of thy tabrets and of thy pipes was prepared in thee in the day that thou wast created.
(Ezekiel 28:13, KJV)

He was embedded with diamonds, beryl, onyx, and every precious stone that you could imagine. He would reflect the glory of God and he was built to praise.

ORIGIN OF THE EVIL ONE

The Hebrew word that was used for "pipes" could also be used for "settings". That is why I believe that his vocals were already "set" as an instrument to worship God when he spoke.

Lucifer didn't have to look for someone to play the organ so that he would sing the doxology. He was the doxology. And that doxology was created as an anointed cherub in Ezekiel 28:14:

> *You were an anointed guardian cherub. I placed you; you were on the holy mountain of God; in the midst of the stones of fire you walked.*

He was created not molded, created as a being to praise God, to reflect the glory of God. This being walked amongst the fiery stones of God, and fire represents the presence and power, the manifest presence of Almighty God. He was essentially created to be the worship leader of heaven.

This being, this cherub, was anointed and called above all other cherubs to walk amongst the fiery flame, have the presence of God and reflect the glory of God, and give praise forth in the way that he was created. From this great pipe organ that was within him would flow praise for God 24/7.

This is how Lucifer, who later became Satan, was created: as a cherub, an angel, a being created solely for God's use and nothing else.

In Ezekiel 28:15, we learn what he now has become.

> *You were blameless in your ways from the day you were created, till unrighteousness was found in you. In the abundance of your trade*

ORIGIN OF THE EVIL ONE

you were filled with violence in your midst, and you sinned; so I cast you as a profane thing from the mountain of God, and I destroyed you, O guardian cherub, from the midst of the stones of fire. Your heart was proud because of your beauty; you corrupted your wisdom for the sake of your splendor. I cast you to the ground; I exposed you before kings, to feast their eyes on you. By the multitude of your iniquities, in the unrighteousness of your trade you profaned your sanctuaries; so I brought fire out from your midst; it consumed you, and I turned you to ashes on the earth in the sight of all who saw you. All who know you among the peoples are appalled at you; you have come to a dreadful end and shall be no more forever.
(Ezekiel 28:15-19)

This being had a will to do as he pleased. He was created to praise our God, but he turned away from God. God created Satan just like He created you and me: to worship and praise Him, but with a free will to turn from Him if we wish.

CHAPTER 7

Free Will

Our God could have created us all as a bunch of automatons that would forcefully repeat, "I praise you, Lord; I praise you, Lord," but He didn't do that.

For you to have a genuine love for God, there must be an operation of free will.

You cannot force your children to love you. You can only act in love towards them and hope that they will choose to love you in return. A programed love isn't love at all, is it?

God created us with free will so that we could choose to love and give God praise, or not.

Satan's sin was rebellion against the will of God and an exercise of his free will. Satan rebelled by using open slander against God amid the stones of fire. He chose to plant the seeds of rebellion against Almighty God, his Creator. On the one hand, Satan gave Him praise. And on the other hand, he was saying, "Can you believe what God did? Well, He must really think He's something to create us all just to praise Him. He must have a real pride problem, because He created us all just to give Him 24/7 praise."

He convinced a third of the angels that he was right, and they followed him in this open rebellion against Almighty God.

We see that in Revelation 12:4a:

His tail swept down a third of the stars of heaven and cast them to the earth.

FREE WILL

And in verse 7:

> *Now war arose in heaven, Michael and his angels fighting against the dragon. And the dragon and his angels fought back, but he was defeated, and there was no longer any place for them in heaven. And the great dragon was thrown down, that ancient serpent, who is called the devil and Satan, the deceiver of the whole world—he was thrown down to the earth, and his angels were thrown down with him.*
> *(Revelation 12:7-9)*

Satan and his angels were cast out of the very presence of Almighty God for the sin of treason.

CHAPTER 8

Focus

So as we study this enemy and his hosts, the fallen angels, we educate ourselves so that we can come out from a place of ignorance and move into a place of knowledge, where we can begin to effectively live our lives in victory over this enemy.

With that being said, we cannot lose our focus. Our focus should always be on Jesus Christ and the sacrifice that He has made for us. Our allegiance as followers of Christ is to Him and to Him alone.

Let's look at Luke 10 where Jesus gives us some perspective:

> *The seventy returned again with joy, saying, Lord, even the devils are subject to us through your name. And He said unto them, I beheld Satan as lightning fall from heaven. Behold, I give unto you power to tread on serpents and scorpions, over all the power of the enemy, and nothing shall by any means hurt you. Notwithstanding, nevertheless, don't rejoice in this, that the spirits are subject unto you, but rather rejoice because your names are written in heaven. (Luke 10:17-20, KJV)*

Jesus, the One who was present at creation and saw Satan fall from heaven, has given you and I authority over all the power of the enemy.

We must know our enemy; we must know our authority over him and we

FOCUS

***must remember whom we serve. And
that is Jesus Christ and Him alone.***

James instructed believers to resist the devil; submission to God naturally means resistance to the devil.

James wrote this exhortation because some of the believers to whom he was writing wanted to be "friends of the world", whose ruler is the devil. Heavenly wisdom is the means of resisting Satan's influence. Just as Jesus combatted the temptations of Satan in the wilderness by marshaling the truth of the word of God against him, so too can the believer.

***One of the tactics of the enemy is to take
the truth and twist it into falsehood.***

For example, Satan sometimes influences a Christian to think something like this: "I can be a faithful Christian and not be a part of a local church." That's the devil's doctrine. And you know what? There is an element of truth in that thought; one can still be a Christian and not attend church, but one cannot be a faithful Christian obeying His Savior by doing that.

The Bible clearly exhorts believers:

> *...to stir up one another to love and good
> works, not neglecting to meet together, as is the
> habit of some, but encouraging one another,
> and all the more as you see the Day drawing
> near. (Hebrews 10:24-25)*

The devil's doctrines are corruptions of the truth, and that is why they are so insidious. We must discern the truth as it is revealed in Scripture.

FOCUS

When Paul wrote about standing against the wiles of the devil, he exhorted Christians to be sure that they are wearing the belt of truth which is the world of God. If we are to avoid being deceived by the enemy, we must know the truth revealed in the pages of our Bibles.

CHAPTER 9

Rejoice

When Christ sent out the seventy-two to every town and place where He Himself was about to go, He gave them power to heal the sick and the authority to cast out demons. When they returned, Jesus told them not to "rejoice in this, that the spirits are subjected to you, but rejoice that your names are written in the heavens" (Luke 10:20).

The same truth should cause you joy as well.

Rejoice that Jesus Christ has come and paid the price for your sin.

Because Jesus paid the price for your sin, you can be forgiven and go to heaven and not go to hell. Having your sins forgiven means that you will not walk in separation from God, but be filled with the Holy Spirit and have a renewed life in victory that overcomes the enemy. Rejoice in this if you know Christ today.

No human being can ever measure up to God's standard of perfection necessary to be in His presence for eternity. Because we are all sinners, we fall short of the glory of God and deserve His condemnation. It is only by turning from our sins and placing our trust in the work of Jesus Christ on the cross where He satisfied the wrath of God and paid for our sins that can we be saved.

That is why we proclaim faith in Jesus Christ. We are saved by faith in Him and the grace of God.

One is either under the condemnation of God, or he is a born-again believer.

REJOICE

For God so loved the world, that he gave his only Son, that whoever believes in him should not perish but have eternal life. (John 3:16)

There's a curse upon your life outside of Jesus Christ. But there's salvation for those who believe. Jesus promised that whoever puts his full trust in Christ shall not perish (that's eternal death, eternal separation from God), but have everlasting life.

If you don't know what to say to God, pray a prayer to Him like this:

Father, I'm a sinner. And I come to you in Jesus' name. I recognize that I have sinned many times against your will and ask that you would forgive all my sins through Jesus Christ. I believe that Jesus paid my debt of sin on the cross when He died in my place. I place my trust in Christ alone for the forgiveness of my sins and the gift of eternal life. In Jesus' name. Amen.

Jesus is the only one that can set you free from the eternal penalty of death. Therefore, put your trust in Him and you shall be saved, delivered, and removed from the curse.

CHAPTER 10

The Names of the Evil One

2 Corinthians 2:11 says:

...so that we would not be outwitted by Satan; for we are not ignorant of his designs.

Paul was pointing out the importance of obeying the word of God so that believers would not give the devil an opportunity to do evil. Paul had earlier counseled the church in Corinth to remove from its membership a man who was having sexual relations with his father's wife. The church had removed him, and the man had then repented of his sin.

The church was hesitating to restore him into fellowship. So, Paul warned them of the possible consequences of their not welcoming him back into fellowship even though he had turned from his sin. The verb translated "to defraud" means to take advantage of someone, to deceive them. Paul's plea was that they should at once restore the repentant offender to their fellowship, because if they did not, Satan would take advantage of it to do injury to him and the church.

Satan is mentioned over 200 times in the word of God under many different names. We are going to reveal the characteristics of the evil one through an examination of his names that are found in the word of God.

Now, for us in America today, names do not have the same weight that they did in biblical times. We are named at birth, and usually named after a relative, or the name is picked because our parents like the way it sounds.

THE NAMES OF THE EVIL ONE

It wasn't always this way, however.

Back in the days of the Bible, people were named for more specific reasons. Some of those reasons would be due to a character in a person's life, or a life-changing event that would be a cause of change to the name of a person.

Jesus' name, Emmanuel, means "God is with us." That's Matthew 1:23. The name "Jesus" was given to Mary by the angel Gabriel, and it also has meaning; it means Savior. Matthew 1:21b says:

> *For He shall save His people from their sins.*
> *(KJV)*

In the Old Testament, Abraham was originally called Abram, and that name had significance; Abram meant "exalted father". But when his name got changed to Abraham, it had a different meaning. "Abraham" means "father of a great multitude". And you'll see that from Abraham came the beginning of the people called the Hebrews.

Jacob's name means "supplanter" or "liar". Thanks, Mom, for giving me a name that means liar! When Jacob wrestled with the angel and won, his name was changed to Israel, meaning "he who prevails with God". In that case, it was a significant event that resulted in the change of his name.

Now, the names of the evil one create a picture of his position in the spiritual world and an understanding of his character traits. We're going to look at seventeen names that the Bible gives to the evil one.

CHAPTER 11

The Devil's Names

Satan was one of the mighty angels that God created. There were a number of notable angels, many of which you have probably heard of before. Michael seems to have been in charge of the military aspects of God's domain. Then there's Gabriel, he seems to have been in charge of telecommunications in heaven, because we see him go to Zacharias and announce the birth of John the Baptist. Scripture reports that he also went to Mary and told her she was with the child of the Holy Spirit, and he told her to name her child "Jesus". In the book of Daniel, we see Gabriel come and help Daniel understand the visions that God had given to him.

One of Satan's names shows his position in the spiritual realm. That name is "the adversary".

> *So I would have younger widows marry, bear children, manage their households, and give the adversary no occasion for slander.*
> *(1 Timothy 5:14)*

He is our opposer. He is the one that is opposed to the will of God. He is the adversary, he is an enemy, he is a foe, and he has enmity in his heart towards God and believers. He doesn't have a good thing to say about you if you call on the name of Christ.

The adversary doesn't have a good thing to say about God because God has sealed his doom in the end, and the adversary is not happy about it.

THE DEVIL'S NAMES

Second, we see the name of Satan in Revelation 12:9 and Luke 10:18:

And the great dragon was thrown down, that ancient serpent, who is called the devil and Satan, the deceiver of the whole world—he was thrown down to the earth, and his angels were thrown down with him. (Revelation 12:9)

And he said to them, "I saw Satan fall like lightning from heaven." (Luke 10:18)

Satan; that name shows us that he is the "adversary" of God and of God's people and the "accuser" of the brethren.

This is what the Hebrew noun שָׂטָן means. The Greek noun Σατανᾶς is a transliteration of the Hebrew with the same meaning.

Thirdly, he is an enemy.

...the enemy that sowed them is the devil. (Matthew 13:39, KJV)

Behold, I have given to you power to tread on serpents and scorpions, and over all the power the enemy, and nothing shall by any means harm you. (Luke 10:19, KJV)

Satan is a spirit being who hates you and hates God and wishes to injure you, your church, your people, and anything good; he is the enemy of all that is good.

And finally, there is the term "devil":

And the great dragon was thrown down, that ancient serpent, who is called the devil and

THE DEVIL'S NAMES

Satan, the deceiver of the whole world—he was thrown down to the earth, and his angels were thrown down with him. (Revelation 12:9)

Be sober-minded; be watchful. Your adversary the devil prowls around like a roaring lion, seeking someone to devour. (1 Peter 5:8)

The Greek word here is διάβολος, which means "false accuser" or "slanderer".

40

CHAPTER 12

God of This World

So what we've seen here is that the devil is an enemy of God and believers.

Now, we're going to look at his position in the spiritual realm, and see that he has a high-ranking position as a promoter of evil. He is the god of this world. In 2 Corinthians 4:4 we learn:

In their case the god of this world has blinded the minds of the unbelievers, to keep them from seeing the light of the gospel of the glory of Christ, who is the image of God.

The Apostle John wrote of the world which "lies in wickedness" (1 John 5:19), referring to those who are opposed to God worship the spirit of hate and falsehood and selfishness. In doing this, they make a god of the devil.

The people who don't believe in Jesus Christ are under the power of this one called the god of this world, and he blinds them to the gospel.

When believers worship in the presence of God, read our Bibles and pray and fellowship with one another, we sometimes forget that there are so many around us who are opposed to God and instead in fellowship with evil.

These people continue in rebellion against God because the god of this world, the prince of darkness, the adversary of man, has blinded them to the truth of the gospel. After all, he does not want them to be saved. He wants them to continue in spiritual darkness where they are. He wants them to be ignorant of the truth of God's word. He wants them to be ignorant and stay ignorant of his power and influence in this world.

Now, some people say the devil does not exist, that the devil is not real or is just an idea preachers use to have power over ignorant people. These people are wrong.

You can't cause Satan to cease to exist by pretending that he doesn't.

There are also false teachers and false prophets prevalent in the church today—men (and women) who don't preach the gospel. Some don't believe in the virgin birth. Some don't believe that the death of Jesus Christ provided a substitutionary atonement for sin. Some deny the truth of the Trinity; they don't believe in the Father, Son, and Holy Spirit. Some don't believe that the Bible is God's word and that every word of it is true. These are the spirits of antichrist who are following the devil.

The devil rules this world in the minds of those who do not believe. I'm telling you, he's got his people in the pulpits of the churches who do not believe the gospel of Jesus Christ. Christians should be very wary of these men; every New Testament book warns the followers of Christ that these false teachers will arise seeking only to benefit themselves by fleecing the sheep.

The devil is a royal dignitary of evil; he is the prince of this world.

Look to John 12:31:

GOD OF THIS WORLD

Now is the judgment of this world; now will the ruler of this world be cast out.

The devil has power in the political realm. The devil is a ruler in the political realm of the world system that we live in because he wants to impact culture in an evil way. One way to do that is to influence a country's leadership.

Satan is a prince; he holds a top rank. He is a chief, a magistrate, and the ruler over our world.

Do you ever wonder why our earth is so screwed up? Do you ever wonder why there are so many people being killed, why abortion is legal in this country, why Christian people are be putting down and why there's so little morality anywhere around us?

It's because the devil has so much influence in the culture in which we live.

CHAPTER 13

Pride

Satan is the king over the children of pride.

Pride is the root of all sin. It is the one thing that brings sin into a person's life. It is the root sin that caused the fall in the Garden of Eden.

Think about when the devil tempted Eve in the Garden of Eden. He told her that God was a liar and that she should eat the fruit that God told her not to eat because she would die if she ate it. She listened to the devil and took the fruit and ate it, disobeying God. She desired it and thought she would be like God; pride rose in her.

Some people are subjects in the devil's kingdom. It' s not just made up of demons. Paul wrote about "the sons of disobedience" in Ephesians 2 who follow "the course of this world." They are the ones who do not serve God or honor the name of Christ but follow Satan even if they do not believe he exists.

Now, let's dig in and discuss the personality of the devil. Let's consider the names that describe Satan's character.

First, we see him called "the wicked one" in 1 John 5:18.

> *We know that everyone who has been born of God does not keep on sinning, but he who was born of God protects him, and the evil one does not touch him.*

Satan is not evil by mistake; rather, he is evil by choice. He is contrary to God's moral law.

PRIDE

The Bible teaches that there is no possibility of redemption for the devil. He is purely, totally completely wicked.

Satan would kill a week-old baby without hesitation or remorse. He will take your children and turn them into drug addicts and send them down the pit when they take a gun and blow their heads off, and he would have a party. This is a wicked being. What he wants for you is your destruction. He's ticked off that his time is short. He knows where he's going, and he wants to take you with him. He is a liar. Jesus stated that in John 8:44:

> *You are of your father the devil, and your will is to do your father's desires. He was a murderer from the beginning, and does not stand in the truth, because there is no truth in him. When he lies, he speaks out of his own character, for he is a liar and the father of lies.*

Satan was a murderer from the beginning. He does not stand for the truth because there is no truth in him. He is a liar and he is the father of liars.

A person who knowingly utters falsehood, that is, declares to another as a fact what he knows is not true, is a liar following in the footsteps of the father of lies. He knows the truth and chooses not to recognize it. Satan chooses to go against God's truth and chooses to lie, meaning you can't believe anything that comes out of his mouth or the mouths of any of his demons.

All you can believe about Satan is that he lies.

PRIDE

On the other hand, the only thing that you can always believe to be the truth is that the Bible is the divinely inspired word of God.

CHAPTER 14

A Tempter

Satan is also a tempter.

When the devil came to Jesus, we read that he tempted Christ in Matthew 4:3:

> *And the tempter came and said to him, "If you are the Son of God, command these stones to become loaves of bread."*

> *For this cause when I could no longer forbear, I sent to know your faith, lest by some means the tempter had tempted you, and our labor might be in vain. (1 Thessalonians 3:5, KJV)*

The one who tempts incites an evil act. To influence someone to do something wrong by presenting arguments that are plausible or convincing or by the offer of some pleasure, or apparent advantage is the inducement. This is exactly what Satan does.

Satan will encourage you to sin, saying things like, "Pilfer this money because it will end your financial bind. Buy this, and you'll be happy. Have sex with somebody outside your marriage. You deserve it. You've been denied all these years, and you deserve a little bit of pleasure."

Now here's the thing: the will lie to you, he will tempt you, he will take from you, and then he will accuse you before God. Revelation 12:10 says:

> *And I heard a loud voice saying in heaven, Now is come salvation and strength in the kingdom of our God and the power of His Christ, for the*

A TEMPTER

> *accuser of our brethren is cast down, which accused them before God day and night.*
> *(Revelation 12:10, KJV)*

Now we can find some satisfaction here because this is what's going to happen to the devil. He's going to be cast down; he's going to be put into the lake of fire.

We can see the way Satan operates by accusing God's children in the oldest book of the Old Testament, the book of Job.

God loved Job; Job was a blameless and upright man, one who feared God and turned away from evil. He always did the right thing. He was a faithful example to his children, showing them how a godly person obeys the Lord.

> *Then Satan answered the Lord and said, "Does Job fear God for no reason? Have you not put a hedge around him and his house and all that he has, on every side? You have blessed the work of his hands, and his possessions have increased in the land. But stretch out your hand and touch all that he has, and he will curse you to your face."*
> *(Job 1:9-11)*

That's what the devil does to you as well. He brings charges against you before your heavenly Father. He is the accuser of the brethren.

When you find an evil thought coming into your mind against a brother or sister in Christ, you better check yourself to see from whom that came.

Chances are it came from the devil himself.

CHAPTER 15

A Thief

Satan is a thief.

John 10:10 says:

> *The thief comes only to steal and kill and destroy. I came that they may have life and have it abundantly.*

He is one who secretly and unlawfully takes the goods or properties of another. The thief takes the property of another privately.

Look into the character of this being. He steals from you when you're not looking. He takes from you when you're unaware.

He takes the things that mean something to you by lying to you. He comes to you as a wolf in sheep's clothing, and comes in the back door and steals the very things that you need for life. Then, he zips out the door, and you don't even know he was there.

The thief does not come except to steal and to kill and destroy you.

We cannot even begin to fathom the plans against us, the church, and our families. So, we must look at what Jesus taught:

> *All who came before me are thieves and robbers, but the sheep did not listen to them. I am the door. If anyone enters by me, he will be saved and will go in and out and find pasture.*

A THIEF

(John 10:8-9)

We must look to Christ as our salvation, and ignore the thief that comes to kill and destroy us. We must claim our God-given authority and reject this thief and his temptations.

CHAPTER 16

Angel of Light

Satan comes as an angel of light. 2 Corinthians 11:14:

And no wonder, for even Satan disguises himself as an angel of light.

He comes disguised as an angel of light. This might be the most important point in the whole lesson; he disguises himself as an angel of light.

The devil doesn't have any problem doing this. Do you know why? Because that's how he was made. He's only going back to how he was made. He's simply putting on the appearance of how God made him in the beginning. He puts on some deception; he transforms himself. He changes his appearance and form and disguises himself so that you would not know it is him.

He acts as though he is still an angel of light to deceive you and destroy the church of Jesus Christ. His purpose is to blind and take as many people to hell with him as he possibly can.

If you are a believer, you need to know this. We believe in the security of the believer. If you're a believer, then you have saving faith in Christ. If that describes you, that means you trust God with your very life and soul. You have faith in Christ and your fellowship is in Christ.

That means you read your Bible and you pray, and you spend time with God regularly, communicating with Him, and letting His Holy Spirit guide you as you follow after Him.

ANGEL OF LIGHT

That doesn't mean that you'll be perfect and always do the right thing. Nor does it mean that you'll never make a mistake and never sin. But if you have Christ in your heart, and you serve God and do right, and you fellowship with Him, and you have faith in Him and you follow after Him, then there is no need to fear. Remember what God has promised us:

> *And I am sure of this, that he who began a good work in you will bring it to completion at the day of Jesus Christ. (Philippians 1:6)*

God's promise is that if He begins the good work of salvation in a person, He will bring it to its completion so that the person will spend eternity with Him.

Now, if you do not know Christ, if you are not born again, then you should fear His righteous judgment. The Bible says, "whoever does not obey the Son shall not see life, but the wrath of God remains on him." The one whom we describe today is the god of those who do not know Christ. He rules and reigns in their lives.

You don't have to get good enough. You don't have to come to Christ having put your life in order. Jesus died when you were a sinner, and He died to pay your debt of sin so that you can be forgiven and brought into the family of God.

Once you realize that you are a sinner before a holy God, that there's none righteous, no, not one, then the next thing is to know that God's remedy for sin is the gift of God is eternal life through Jesus Christ.

ANGEL OF LIGHT

Jesus Christ is eternal life and whosoever shall call upon the name of the Lord shall be saved.

CHAPTER 17

Biblical Influence

Now, we are going to discuss the hosts of evil.

I have told you this before, but it bears repeating: there is only one authoritative, reliable source for truth regarding the devil and his demons. It is the word of God.

We must not allow our beliefs to be formed through any other source than the Bible.

A Google search I did for the word "demons" reveals 5,280,000 hits. A quick survey of our local video store actually showed that in the new release section, there were at least 68 titles that were blatantly demonic. There were only around five that were obviously Christian.

Movies, TV shows, documentaries, and video games are not reliable sources of spiritual truth. These sources by design create fear to produce a profit. The Bible says in 2 Timothy 1:7:

...for God gave us a spirit not of fear but of power and love and self-control.

The Bible's revelation about the devil, demons, and evil should lead the believer to avoid those things in our culture that glorify evil. The Bible's revelations should encourage the believer to focus on love, joy, peace, patience, kindness, goodness, faithfulness, gentleness, and self-control.

Therefore, if we want strength in this area, we must heed biblical revelation about evil and be very careful of worldly influences in this area.

BIBLICAL INFLUENCE

Our enemy purposely influences ungodly people to promote wickedness through movies and entertainment to influence you, to pollute your mind, and to lead you to question the truth of God's revelation.

In the next few chapters, we will look into the subject of demonic power in three areas:

1. **The origins of demonic power**
2. **The abodes of demons**
3. **The manifestations of demons**

CHAPTER 18

Definitions

A demon biblically is an evil spirit, one opposed to the will of God.

The English word for demon is a transliteration of the Greek word for demon, "daimōn", from the Greek verb "daiesthai" that meant to distribute fortunes.

Now let's explore the origins of demons. They are the devil's angels. We see this in Revelation 12:7-9:

> *Now war arose in heaven, Michael and his angels fighting against the dragon. And the dragon and his angels fought back, but he was defeated, and there was no longer any place for them in heaven. And the great dragon was thrown down, that ancient serpent, who is called the devil and Satan, the deceiver of the whole world—he was thrown down to the earth, and his angels were thrown down with him.*

Satan was cast into the earth and his angels were cast out with him. John was writing about the way that Satan leads mankind into idolatry and religious superstition. This was true of the entire Roman world at the time John wrote the book of Revelation.

The devil's influence continues today as he seeks to seduce people into believing the lie that they do not need the wisdom of God in order to live their lives.

DEFINITIONS

Adam and Eve needed God's direction for their lives even before they sinned. That was why God communicated truth to them.

> **We were created to be beings
> dependent upon God.**

Satan deceives the people of the world into thinking that they can get along just fine in the world without God or His wisdom. That is his chief deception. It began in the garden and it continues today.

> *But when the Pharisees heard it, they said, "It is only by Beelzebub, the prince of demons, that this man casts out demons." Knowing their thoughts, he said to them, "Every kingdom divided against itself is laid waste, and no city or house divided against itself will stand. And if Satan casts out Satan, he is divided against himself. How then will his kingdom stand?*
> *(Matthew 12:24-26)*

Jesus had just delivered a demon-possessed man; all the people were rightfully amazed, but the Pharisees charged Jesus with casting out the demon by the power of Beelzebub, the prince of demons. Jesus pointed out to them that if Satan casts out Satan, he is divided against himself. How then shall his kingdom stand?

> **Satan has a kingdom and his kingdom
> consists of the things that a kingdom
> must have. It has a king, it has nobles,
> and it has subjects.**

DEFINITIONS

The demons who serve Satan are malevolent; they are wishing evil or harm to others. You can't appeal to their good nature, because they do not have one.

Mark tells us about an incident in the life of Jesus that illustrates well just how evil demons are.

> *Night and day among the tombs and on the mountains he was always crying out and cutting himself with stones. And when he saw Jesus from afar, he ran and fell down before him. And crying out with a loud voice, he said, "What have you to do with me, Jesus, Son of the Most High God? I adjure you by God, do not torment me." For he was saying to him, "Come out of the man, you unclean spirit!" And Jesus asked him, "What is your name?" He replied, "My name is Legion, for we are many."*
> *(Mark 5:5-9)*

So, what we have here is a picture of a personality. The demon can communicate, he can talk, he can answer questions, and he can lie, but he has no corporality.

The demon himself did not have a body, but he was inhabiting the man's body and destroying the man in the process.

Now consider verse 10:

> *And he begged him earnestly not to send them out of the country. Now a great herd of pigs was feeding there on the hillside, and they begged him, saying, "Send us to the pigs; let us enter them."*

DEFINITIONS

These evil demons were destroying this man's life by making him cut himself with stones. Demons have malevolent personalities, and that was the reason Jesus commanded them to leave the man's body and to enter the bodies of the pigs.

Demons have varying degrees of wickedness, and you can see that expressed in Matthew 12:45:

Then it goes and brings with it seven other spirits more evil than itself, and they enter and dwell there, and the last state of that person is worse than the first.

The Greek word translated "evil" means hurtful, especially morally wicked or vicious.

Now, as we discussed earlier, a third of the angels joined Satan in his rebellion and thus were expelled from heaven by God.

Exactly how many demons does the devil have at his disposal, you may wonder?

Well, for the answer to that, we can look to the prophecies given to us in Daniel chapter seven.

As I looked, thrones were placed, and the Ancient of Days took his seat; his clothing was white as snow, and the hair of his head like pure wool; his throne was fiery flames; its wheels were burning fire. A stream of fire issued and came out from before him; a thousand thousands served him, and ten thousand times ten thousand stood before him; the court sat in judgment, and the books were opened. I looked

DEFINITIONS

then because of the sound of the great words that the horn was speaking. And as I looked, the beast was killed, and its body destroyed and given over to be burned with fire. As for the rest of the beasts, their dominion was taken away, but their lives were prolonged for a season and a time. (Daniel 7:9-12)

The demons of course are not the thousand thousands that serve Christ, but part of the ten thousand times ten thousand.

Now, if we assume that those numbers are the angels, that's still more than one hundred million demons that are loosed in the world to do the devil's bidding.

That is why it is so important that we are aware of their existence; they are everywhere. If we do not allow them to have power over us, but instead bask in the truth of God's word, we can be victorious in God's name.

CHAPTER 19

Of the World

The Bible reveals everything we need to know about Satan and demons. Jesus talked more about demons than He did angels, and had more to say about hell than He did about heaven.

Jesus knew how important it is that you know that there's a hell. Jesus and His apostles wanted believers to be aware of the danger of demonic influence and to stand against it.

In Ephesians 2, Paul reminded believers,

And you were dead in the trespasses and sins in which you once walked, following the course of this world, following the prince of the power of the air, the spirit that is now at work in the sons of disobedience... (Ephesians 2:1-2)

Satan is called the prince of the power of the air.

He rules in this domain between heaven and earth. Some call this the second heaven. The first heaven is the atmosphere around our planet, and the third heaven is the dwelling place of God.

CHAPTER 20

Chapter 20: Heaven

I must go on boasting. Though there is nothing to be gained by it, I will go on to visions and revelations of the Lord. I know a man in Christ who fourteen years ago was caught up to the third heaven—whether in the body or out of the body I do not know, God knows. And I know that this man was caught up into paradise—whether in the body or out of the body I do not know, God knows—and he heard things that cannot be told, which man may not utter.

There is a spiritual place called heaven. Paul says he knew a man (whether it was a spiritual experience or was actually in the body he said he could not tell) who had entered into paradise and heard things that it was not lawful for a man to utter.

Paul was caught up to where God's throne is. That's the place where you and I are going to go when we leave this earth. That's the place that we get to go to when we come to know Jesus as our Savior. That's the place where there are no more tears. That's the place where there'll be no more crying, and that's the place where I will be known, even as I am known. That's the place where there'll be no more secrets. That's the place where we won't be confused anymore and everything wrong will be made right, once and for all.

Remember we are just passing through this earth. My address is going to be changed. It's going to be heaven.

OF THE WORLD

    I'm looking forward to that. But I have some work to do down here. And I'm hoping you'll do this work with me. We're going to take as many people to heaven with us as we possibly can. We're going to decrease the number of people going to hell. We're going to glorify God, hallelujah; we're going to give Him praise because He so honestly deserves it from us.

CHAPTER 21

Order

Consider what the Bible says about the ranking of demonic beings.

According to Ephesians 6:12, demons are ranked in orders or ranks:

> *For we do not wrestle against flesh and blood, but against the rulers, against the authorities, against the cosmic powers over this present darkness, against the spiritual forces of evil in the heavenly places.*

These spiritual forces of evil are not without their enemies. Jesus is far above all other principalities and powers. Now, He's not a little bit above. He's not kind of above. He's completely, totally, awesomely, incredibly, above all rule and authority and power and dominion. He is above every name that is named not only in the current age but in the age that is to come.

> *For by him all things were created, in heaven and on earth, visible and invisible, whether thrones or dominions or rulers or authorities— all things were created through him and for him. And he is before all things, and in him all things hold together. And he is the head of the body, the church. He is the beginning, the firstborn from the dead, that in everything he might be preeminent. (Colossians, 1:16-18)*

In the ranks far below Christ, there are eight different ranks of demons that Paul mentioned in these three passages.

ORDER

1. ἀρχῆς – this word means "chief", or in first place. This word was used to describe those in a position of political power, e.g., see Titus 3:1, a passage which describes human rulers or magistrates. Paul used the term to refer to angelic "rulers."

2. ἐξουσίας – the word means "authority". The word is used either of humans or demons who have authority.

3. **δυνάμεως** – the word means "power". The word is used either of humans or demons who have power, but slightly less than the previous ranking.

4. **κυριότητος** – this word means "dominion", whether a human or angelic one.

5. **κοσμοκράτορας τοῦ σκότους τούτου** – this word means literally "world-rulers". The word was used both to describe human rulers and of the angel of death. These are world-rulers of this darkness, referring to evil demons in the world.

6. **πνευματικὰ τῆς πονηρίας** – this word means "spirit". Here it is an adjective, "spiritual", but not spiritual in a Christian sense. In this usage, Paul meant "spiritual" beings or forces of "evil".

7. **θρόνοι** – this word means "thrones".

8. **κυριότητες** – the word is plural here and refers to ones who possess dominion, whether human or angelic. This is the same word as #4. The only difference is that #4 refers to the dominion that a ruler holds, and here it refers to the ones holding the dominion.

Paul does not place these ranks in any particular sequence.

ORDER

For example, ἀρχῆς appears first in the list in Ephesians 1:21 and 6:12, but it is third in the list in Colossians 1:16. ἐξουσίας is second in the list in Ephesians 1:21 and 6:12, but it is fourth in the list in Colossians 1:16.

δυνάμεως and κυριότητος appear in Ephesians 1:21, but they are not mentioned in Ephesians 6:12 or Colossians 1:16.

Some have argued that Paul lists the demonic powers in descending order in Ephesians 1:21, a theory with which I agree. I do not think that a Bible student can be dogmatic about whether Paul placed these all in a particular order since each list he gives is so different.

> ***What you can conclude is that there are eight different orders of demons who have different functions or roles, and that there's always an order to everything.***

I think it's helpful sometimes to think about the lists that Paul makes of demons like a grocery list. When you make a grocery list, do you make that list in order of importance? Do you make a list of things in order that you find them in the store? No, probably not – unless you're much more organized than pretty much everyone else in the world! You probably make it in sections: produce, fresh vegetables, meat, canned goods, etc. When Paul offers us this list of demons, he doesn't necessarily offer them to us in order of importance, but in divisions that make sense. These demons have powers in different areas.

CHAPTER 22

Control

Satan seeks to influence people to oppose the will of God. His goal is clearly to destroy that which God has created for His glory.

> ***Satan and his demons influence people to engage in evil rather than righteousness.***

However, it's important to know that not all evil in the world is directly attributable to Satan. People are quite capable of sinning with no help from Satan. Because humans have a sinful nature, they can make bad choices and do evil all on their own. Not all suffering is attributed to the devil and his horde of demons either – humans can be responsible for our own suffering.

> ***People have sinful desires like lust, for example, that they can act on without any help from Satan at all! Be careful not to give too much credit to demons.***

While not all sickness can be attributed to demonic activity, the Bible does reveal that demons can cause sickness and disease. They were particularly active on earth during Jesus' public ministry in this way, as the New Testament gospels reveal.

First, we see in Matthew 9:32 and 33 that deafness and dumbness can be a result of demonic spirit.

> *As they were going away, behold, a demon-oppressed man who was mute was brought to him. And when the demon had been cast out, the*

mute man spoke. And the crowds marveled, saying, "Never was anything like this seen in Israel."

Jesus demonstrated His power over the demonic again and again. He cast the demon out and the mute spoke.

Blindness can be caused by demon power. Look at Matthew 12:22:

Then a demon-oppressed man who was blind and mute was brought to him, and he healed him, so that the man spoke and saw.

Who's got the power? Jesus.

Matthew 17:15 records that demons can be the cause of epileptic seizures:

Lord, have mercy on my son, for he has seizures and he suffers terribly. For often he falls into the fire, and often into the water.

Now, I have a personal story to relate about the influence that demons can have on a person. About 20 some years ago, a woman that I know very well was put into the Logansport insane asylum. She was put in for a nervous breakdown. This person saw demons underneath the masks of the faces of the people around her.

She was told that her problem was that she had a fixation on religion, and she needed to lose her fixation on religion. They took her Bible away. They drugged her to the point that she could barely think.

CONTROL

In moments of lucidity, she would quote Scripture, only little parts that she had memorized; maybe John 3:16, whatever she could remember. And she realized the only way she was going to get out of there was to stop taking the drugs that they were giving her because she could not think. And she also realized that the only way she was going to get out of there was through the power of God. She began to flush her drugs down the toilet and begin to tell them what they wanted to hear in the counseling sessions, namely that she had lost her fixation with religion.

Eventually, they gave her Bible back, and she said that's when she started to get better, because she started to read the word of God. She began to put into her mind the things that renewed her mind. She has been normal and well for 20 years since; although she had been under the influence of demonic power, she was set free through the word of God. Amen.

Demons can cause people to think a lot of crazy things.

Mark 5:3-4 tells us the story of the demons that caused supernatural strength for a demoniac in Gadara. It says that chains had been pulled apart by this man and the shackles broken in pieces, and no one could subdue him. This supernatural strength was destructive to the man. Ruin is always what Satan does; nothing the devil does in people's lives is for their benefit.

Demons can also influence a person to commit suicide. In Matthew 17:15, a man pleaded to the Lord to have mercy on his son, for the boy had seizures and he suffered terribly. For often he fell into the fire, and often into the water. The demonic spirit that was in him was trying to burn him to death

CONTROL

or drown him to death. Suicide can be the result of demon spirits.

Sexual temptation and lust can also be motivated by demons. John 8:44 says:

> *You are of your father the devil, and your will is to do your father's desires. He was a murderer from the beginning, and does not stand in the truth, because there is no truth in him. When he lies, he speaks out of his own character, for he is a liar and the father of lies.*

The Apostle Paul wrote to the believers in Rome to remind them that they could choose to walk in righteousness because of what Christ had accomplished in their lives:

> *Do not present your members to sin as instruments for unrighteousness, but present yourselves to God as those who have been brought from death to life, and your members to God as instruments for righteousness. For sin will have no dominion over you, since you are not under law but under grace.*
> *(Romans 6:13-14)*

General weakness and infirmity can also be demonically caused.

We see in Acts 10:38 how God anointed Jesus of Nazareth with Holy Spirit and with power, who went about doing good and healing all who were oppressed by the devil, for God was with Him.

You see, the Scripture here demonstrates that Christ can deliver from demonic oppression.

CONTROL

Demon spirits are subject to Christ. This biblical revelation about the spiritual powers around us should not bring fear, but lead to trusting Christ, for knowledge of God's truth is power.

He returned with joy, saying, Lord, even the demons are subject. (Luke 10:17)

Now, this is an awesome word. "Subject" means to be subordinate, reflexively to obey, to be put under obedience, to subdue and made subject in subjection to, to submit to. Those demons are made subject to us.

Demons are made subject to those that have faith. This doesn't work for those who "almost" believe. It works for those who put their total and complete trust in Christ. This word is for those of us who have given our very lives and souls to Jesus Christ, and have trusted Him that we won't go to hell, but will go to heaven.

I'm telling you, just warming up a pew on a Sunday morning isn't going to get you there. Being the top dog in the political structure is not going to get you there either. Nor is having a nice suit is not going to do it. You have got to believe in the Lord Jesus Christ, and you shall be saved.

Those who believe shall cast out demons.

Believers in the church today are told to do two things:

1. Stand against the devil.

2. Resist the devil.

Both passages where these instructions are given emphasize that this is done by wielding the word of God. We

CONTROL

resist Satan the way that Jesus did in the wilderness: with the truth of God's word.

We are told to keep our eyes <u>focused on Jesus, not demons</u>.

> *Therefore, since we are surrounded by so great a cloud of witnesses, let us also lay aside every weight, and sin which clings so closely, and let us run with endurance the race that is set before us, looking to Jesus, the founder and perfecter of our faith, who for the joy that was set before him endured the cross, despising the shame, and is seated at the right hand of the throne of God. (Hebrews 12:1-2)*

Too many charismatic teachers encourage looking for demons instead of looking to Jesus.

CHAPTER 23

Believe God's Word

You have to believe the Bible entirely, never just choosing bits and pieces to believe. Never decide that some Scripture applies but other Scriptures don't because you like what one verse says but are offended by something another verse says.

Believe this book is what it claims to be: the actual word of God. Believe that it is truth given by the Holy Spirit from beginning to end, that the very words within it are what God would have you know so that you can faithfully follow Jesus and please Him in all you do.

You will have the strength, power, and wisdom to be able to resist the influence of Satan because you know the word of God and what God expects you to believe and do.

Step up and make a wise decision to believe the Bible. Always choose to live a moral life. What God commands His children to do is to live righteously, doing what is good, just, and pleasing to Him.

Now, God knows full well that we're going to fail. We're going to transgress the will of God and sin. Still, he asks us to obey Him.

God does not ask us just to have a plan, but to actually obey! People can have intentions and never do anything with them. Have you ever heard the proverb, "The road to hell is paved with good intentions"?

BELIEVE GOD'S WORD

Notice carefully the wording of the verse that was quoted after the sentence, 1 John 1:8-9:

If we say we have no sin, we deceive ourselves, and the truth is not in us. If we confess our sins, he is faithful and just to forgive us our sins and to cleanse us from all unrighteousness.

God provides the way to get back into a relationship with Him by confessing our sins. He's faithful and just to forgive our sins, and He will cleanse us from all unrighteousness.

We must demonstrate that we are the people of God, so that people know we are the people of God by how we act towards one another in the world around us.

Jesus said, "You shall know the truth, and the truth will set you free." The sinner finds true freedom—freedom from slavery to sin and from the futility of what this world offers—by knowing Christ. Being made a child of God by the regenerating work of the Holy Spirit, you are enabled to live a life pleasing to the Lord now and assured of being in the presence of god forever because of His gift of eternal life. .

You are here today reading this by divine appointment. God has you reading the truth from the word of God.

CHAPTER 24

God's Power

Now, let's consider God's power over the power of the enemy.

Power to resist Satan comes from knowing the truth of the word of God.

> ***Paul said we are not ignorant of the devil's devices, but that is only true if you know Christ as your Savior.***

Do you know Christ? If you don't know Jesus Christ as your Savior, you cannot possibly resist the influence of the devil in your life.

God is a Being of power, love, and a sound mind. He offers you that love through His word and His truth. The devil would keep you ignorant, but God would have you know the truth and have that truth set you free.

I was a drug addict, and God saved me and put me in the pulpit to preach the gospel. I do it with all I have. God can change your life so that you bring Him glory, too.

> ***You do not need to be oppressed nor influenced by the enemy's foolishness any longer.***

If you are a believer and live a life pleasing to God, you will see many people (including yourself) set free.

People today need to see Christians living according to the word of God demonstrating the change that Jesus makes in a person's life.

GOD'S POWER

There are many throughout the world, including me, who know that freedom, and I want to help you know the freedom as well.

CHAPTER 25

Three Things

We live in an evil world that is filled with deception. The airwaves are filled with it, radio, TV, the movie theaters, and internet are filled with it. So many mediums appeal to the allure of the senses and sexual enticement. The internet is really the culmination of this deception. There's so much information that's just outright lies, incorrect opinions, religious nuts, pornographic predators, etc.

On the internet, it is nearly impossible to tell the difference between the truth and a lie, or fact from opinion. It all plays to the devil's ultimate purpose of confusion.

Now, God has given us a measuring stick by which we can discern the truth from lies, right from wrong, good from bad.

That is His Bible, the word of God, the only verifiable source of truth about the spiritual.

We have begun to look into the evil one and how to overcome him. We have revealed the enemy up to this point, his hosts, and now we are about to expose his tactics and process to deceive the human beings on an individual level.

For the non-Christian, there is a process that is used by the devil in an attempt to keep a person from ever coming to know a saving knowledge of Jesus Christ.

For a Christian, it is a process that attempts to render them completely and permanently ineffectual for the cause of Christ.

THREE THINGS

Alcoholism starts with just one drink, or sip. Drug abuse may start with a seemingly harmless cigarette. Physical abuse of a child or a spouse may start with an improper thought or a raised hand. A suicide may start with the acceptance of the thought of self-pity.

Whatever the problem, it all starts with a seemingly harmless first step.

If curbed or stopped here, it can be changed fairly easily. But if it is allowed to continue unchecked, it can lead to a point where deliverance and intervention may be needed to avert a spiritual and physical disaster. And when it is allowed to develop to the later stages, much knowledge, much faith, and much action may be required to turn the situation around.

There are three things you must learn about deception:

1. The area of deception
2. the nature of deception
3. The process of deception

Follow along with me as I discuss these three things in the next few chapters.

CHAPTER 26

The Battleground

1 Timothy 3:7 states:

Moreover, he must be well thought of by outsiders, so that he may not fall into disgrace, into a snare of the devil.

You may say to me, "I don't believe that the snares of the devil are for the Christian person." Well, I have to tell you, this right here is talking about the church leadership. He is talking of an overseer of the church falling into the snare of the devil.

Now, a snare is a trap for small animals. It is a concealed trap. It is a stationary trap.

Out ahead of us, some snares are laid out for us, and we have to know our enemy and keep our eyeballs peeled as we follow the Spirit to keep our feet out of the snares of the devil. Additionally, we need protection from these traps.

The spiritual battleground that Christians face is dealt with in Ephesians 6:11-12:

Put on the whole armor of God, that you may be able to stand against the schemes of the devil. For we do not wrestle against flesh and blood, but against the rulers, against the authorities, against the cosmic powers over this present darkness, against the spiritual forces of evil in the heavenly places.

Now, the Greek word translated "schemes" means methods. The different wiles of the devil are used to deceive,

THE BATTLEGROUND

trap, enslave, and ruin the souls of men. These are the devil's schemes, methods, and traps that we fight and wrestle with. Ephesians 6:12 refers to spiritual warfare in general, between the saints and the spirit rebels that are the devil's host. The Greek word that is translated "wrestle" referred to a contest between two men in which each endeavored to overpower the other.

> ***This wrestling match, this battleground, is for the souls of men and women, boys and girls.***

The soul is made up of the mind, the will, and the emotions. The mind is the intellect; the thinking processes that are parts of man's mind. Your emotions include your passions, your desires, and your moods. Your will has to do with your decision making, your volition, and your purposeful deciding.

Man was also created with the physicality of the human body. The body is our contact point with our surroundings. These are our senses of touch, taste, smell, hearing, and sight (the five senses). In the born-again person, the body becomes the temple of the Holy Spirit.

One of the important reasons that Christians should seek to be victorious in obeying Christ's word and not giving in to the influence of the devil is because the believer's body is the temple of the Holy Spirit. Notice how the Apostle Paul rebuked the believers in Corinth for their failure to appreciate this truth in 1 Corinthians 6:19:

> *Or do you not know that your body is a temple of the Holy Spirit within you, whom you have from God? You are not your own...*

THE BATTLEGROUND

Your body becomes the temple of the Holy Spirit, the property of God, when you are born again.

Now, this battle of living for the Lord or the devil is won in the thought life. And if we look into Genesis 3:1, we see a tremendous example of this battle.

> *Now the serpent was more crafty than any other beast of the field that the Lord God had made. He said to the woman, "Did God actually say, 'You shall not eat of any tree in the garden'?" And the woman said to the serpent, "We may eat of the fruit of the trees in the garden, but God said, 'You shall not eat of the fruit of the tree that is in the midst of the garden, neither shall you touch it, lest you die.'" But the serpent said to the woman, "You will not surely die. For God knows that when you eat of it your eyes will be opened, and you will be like God, knowing good and evil." (Genesis 3:1-5)*

Be careful when you add to the word of God, because that's what Eve did because God did not say, "lest you touch it." He said, "Don't eat it." And the serpent said in the woman, "You shall not surely die."

This is the devil's method. He did it in the garden, and he is still doing it today; he's going to directly contradict God's word. He is insinuates, "Did God really say that? Did he really? You shall not surely die." Eve bought into it.

Here's the battle for the soul right here:

THE BATTLEGROUND

*For God knows that when you eat of it your
eyes will be opened, and you will be like God,
knowing good and evil. (Genesis 3:5)*

Eve began to reason, "You shall not surely die." It was pleasant to the eyes and a tree desirable to make one wise.

Eve was deceived into thinking that God was withholding something from her and Adam. She failed to realize that God made humans as beings dependent on the wisdom of God for life. In a desire to be wise, she abandoned that dependency on God and took the fruit and ate, and she gave it to Adam. When he ate, the eyes of both were opened, and they knew they were naked, so they sewed fig leaves together and made themselves loincloths.

Satan is subtle, for he is cunning, and he operates undercover. The devil will take a world full of people to hell with him, and they won't even know they're serving him. That's his move.

People that are walking down the street that you encounter throughout your day who don't believe in God are already on the devil's side.

They don't believe in God and they don't believe in the devil, and yet they serve him, but they do not even know it. You may wonder, why do they prosper? Why do they do well? The answer is because the devil doesn't need to mess with them. He's convinced them to live through their flesh.

Satan attacks the soul, intellect and emotions. The devil tries to submit the will of man to him. In the back of your head is the ability to process thoughts and evaluate your

THE BATTLEGROUND

emotions, passions, desires, moods, and will. That is your decision-making process where insight often comes from.

The devil attacks and works within the soul through your intellect and your emotions to try to submit your will. And once he submits your will, your defenses against him are gone.

This is often the case for unbelievers, but for believers, we always have the obligation to resist the devil or to take his stand against the devil and do right.

We are never powerless.

> *Do not present your members to sin as instruments for unrighteousness, but present yourselves to God as those who have been brought from death to life, and your members to God as instruments for righteousness.*
> *(Romans 6:13)*

This battle is won in the thoughts by the exercising of our will. 2 Corinthians 10:3-5 says:

> *For though we walk in the flesh, we are not waging war according to the flesh. For the weapons of our warfare are not of the flesh but have divine power to destroy strongholds. We destroy arguments and every lofty opinion raised against the knowledge of God, and take every thought captive to obey Christ.*

The devil has strongholds in the minds of people, and he wishes to build strongholds in your life, specifically, to build strongholds in your mind. However, the weapons of our

THE BATTLEGROUND

warfare are not carnal. God gives you weapons for the pulling down of strongholds that the devil builds in your mind.

With the power of the word of God on your side, you can defeat the devil. With biblical knowledge of God, bringing every thought into captivity, turning from sin and being obedient to Christ, you can defeat the devil.

CHAPTER 27

The Devil's Methods

Bringing thoughts captive involves an act of the will.

You must bring your thoughts into captivity through an exercise of your will by choosing to obey God.

God knows how we were made. He reveals to us how we were made. He allows us to be free but allows us to have the victory. All we need to do is embrace the strength and empowerment of His Spirit to overcome the wiles of the devil.

Glory to God, this battle is won in the thought life. This is exactly why the devil will do all he can to keep you from prayer and to keep you out of the word of God; because he doesn't want you to be thinking any differently.

You can rise and be the child of God that God has called you to be.

God's purpose for your life is for you to bring God glory in all that you do. Paul said it emphatically in 1 Corinthians 10:31:

So, whether you eat or drink, or whatever you do, do all to the glory of God.

The devil's design for you is to the opposite of this; it is to destroy you. John 10:10 says –

The thief comes only to steal and kill and destroy. I came that they may have life and have it abundantly.

THE DEVIL'S METHODS

The devil's purpose in this world and in your life is to steal what you have that's good, to kill anything that has any value, and to destroy you personally. That is his purpose. And he's pretty good at his job. I look around me and I see people go down that devilish slide every day. It is a subtle slide; it's the devil's slide.

Now, remember, the devil's aim for the Christian is to render you completely ineffective for the cause of Christ.

For the non-Christians, this slide is to keep them from ever coming to know him at all. This slide begins with one step.

The first step is **regression.** Regression means to go backward, to revert to earlier behavior patterns.

Now, many times I've seen people come to know the Lord. I've seen them get excited; I see them get in there; I see them get fired up, and I see them have victory. I see them go forward. I see them doing well. Then, all of a sudden, you'll see them take one minor step backward. I'll see someone at next Wednesday's prayer meeting, or I'll see them next Sunday at church and they've lost that initial excitement about reading their Bible. Perhaps they stop praying. Maybe they just show up with a little less excitement than they used to before.

Even though these are minor changes, they are impactful ones. Maybe they'll start to miss praying with fellow believers or skipping their small group meeting. They say something like, "Hey, I'll just, you know, try to make it to church next Sunday, and I'll get my Bible out tomorrow."

Regression is a backward movement, to revert to earlier behavior patterns.

Once you go back even a little bit, you begin to develop a habit that keeps you from moving forward again. That is the second step, **habit formation**.

What is the counsel of God's word?

What is the Christian to do if he realizes that he is forming bad habits that are not in sync with the way that Christ would have him live?

The Apostle Paul answers these questions in his letter to the Ephesians. In chapter four, he made the point that unbelievers "have given themselves up to sensuality, greedy to practice every kind of impurity." Every follower of Christ has learned something that is crucial to obey, "to put off your old self, which belongs to your former manner of life." That means that the habits that were part of your life before you were born again must go!

You are "to be renewed in the spirit of your minds, and to put on the new self, created after the likeness of God in true righteousness and holiness."

That is, you must develop new habits that please your heavenly Father.

Paul then gave several specific examples of what he meant. He wrote, "Therefore, having put away falsehood, let each one of you speak the truth with his neighbor, for we are members one of another." If you used to lie before you came to Christ, you must now choose not to lie but tell the truth.

THE DEVIL'S METHODS

Paul said, "Let the thief no longer steal, but rather let him labor, doing honest work with his own hands, so that he may have something to share with anyone in need." If you used to steal before you came to Christ, you must now choose not to steal but do honest work.

In other words, the apostle's counsel was to engage in a process of mind renewal—thinking biblically—so that you can form new habits that bring glory to God. You should want to do this so that you "do not grieve the Holy Spirit of God, by whom you were sealed for the day of redemption."

Ephesians 4 ends with this counsel about Christian behavior:

> *Let all bitterness and wrath and anger and clamor and slander be put away from you, along with all malice. Be kind to one another, tenderhearted, forgiving one another, as God in Christ forgave you. (Ephesians 4:31-32)*

Following Paul's directions here means developing godly habits that please God, bring glory to God, and bless others.

The third step is **suppression,** the act of forcefully putting you down, intentionally holding you back. As we continue to move in the direction Satan prefers, we don't recognize this process of suppression. It begins slowly, and then when the suppressive force grows stronger, there begins to be great pressure to keep you from moving in the direction God intends for you to go. This then allows the devil opportunity to begin his sneaky work in a person's life when they begin to move away from Christ.

THE DEVIL'S METHODS

Suppression is actual pressure to keep you from moving in the right direction.

Then there is the fourth step: **depression**. There are a lot of depressed people in the world right now. Depression is a low place and it renders you low in spiritual force.

When you are depressed, you are forced into a place where it's very difficult to get out of a decrease in force or activity.

This leaves many people downward spiral that leads to fewer things of spiritual power and a feeling like they are unable to turn back at this point.

When you get to this point, it's not so subtle anymore.

The next step is **oppression**. This is where we get to a point where things are getting really bad. When you feel oppressed, you are kept down by the cruel and unjust evil use of authority.

If the devil brings you down to this place, it is by the unjust use of stolen authority. But you have by your own will given this power freely over to him.

The only way to get out of this oppression is to actual obey the Holy Spirit.

To free yourself from the power of the devil, you need to embrace the spiritual power only the Holy Spirit can provide. You have to get with the One who went about doing good and healing all who were oppressed by the devil, for Jesus is God.

THE DEVIL'S METHODS

At this point during this oppression stage, it may require the intervention of one who operates in a higher level of authority than you that is willing to intervene on your behalf. There comes a time when the will is lessening and lessening, and the power to resist and turn around and get away becomes such that it's almost impossible to do on your own. That's why there is the body of Christ. That's why there is power in Jesus' name. That's why there are people of faith who know what's going on in the spiritual realm. These people will intervene because of love, and they will help to bring deliverance. But then at that point, there must be a renewal of your will to retain that freedom.

After oppression comes **obsession**. This is to haunt or trouble a mind; to be fixed on a single idea to an unreasonable degree. It is having an obsession with any one thing that can destroy a person's life.

There are good obsessions though. One of them is an obsession with God and Jesus Christ, and love and kindness and goodness; you can be obsessed with these things. I'll say you're doing okay. But there are also terribly demonic obsessions that will destroy your life, and they take your attention and consume you. When you see people who are obsessed with alcohol, they absolutely destroy everything around them, ignore their family, ignore the people around them, and take every dollar that's meant to provide for their families and they spend it on alcohol. They are just absolutely obsessed to the point that they have no willpower to resist their addiction.

And finally, the last step is **possession**. Possession implies ownership, but it can be temporary or permanent. It

THE DEVIL'S METHODS

means to inhabit, control, occupy, and rule by extraneous forces.

This is where a person is just absolutely consumed by the power of the enemy. It often begins in such a subtle way that you may not even notice it happening. Possession then increases in force as you worked your way down this de-evolving downward spiral. You finally get to this end, and there's just no willpower left. At this point, it requires the intervention of one who knows the power of God set a person free.

I knew a lady who was possessed, she didn't even know it. And it required the intervention of those who knew the power of God to get her free so that she could actually serve God and live for Christ. Now her whole family has come to know the Lord. It's a tremendous story of the deliverance through the power that is in the name of Jesus Christ.

CHAPTER 28

God Can Deliver

And at even, when the sun did set, they brought unto him all that were diseased, and them that were possessed with devils. And all the city was gathered together at the door. And he healed many that were sick of divers diseases, and cast out many devils; and suffered not the devils to speak, because they knew him.
(Mark 1:32-34, KJV)

Jesus has the power. Jesus has given us a way out. He has given us the authority to not be under the will of the devil.

Jesus' path to freedom for the person who is lost is to repent of their sin and turn to Him for forgiveness, and then to live a life of faithful obedience.

John 8:32 says:

You shall know the truth, and the truth will set you free. (KJV)

Truth brings what? Freedom.

Jesus forgives a person's sins and gives him eternal life so that he can live for God instead of himself. When this happens, you are made alive and you begin to live by being filled with the Holy Spirit.

Do not be conformed to this world, but be transformed by the renewal of your mind, that by testing you may discern what is the will of

GOD CAN DELIVER

*God, what is good and acceptable and perfect.
(Romans 12:2)*

You have to renew your mind, and you do this through the truth. You do this by the application of the word of God.

When you are thinking biblically, you will behave in a godly way; you will make choices that conform to the will of God. You will be doing what is good, acceptable, and perfect. These three adjectives: good, acceptable, and perfect, describe actions that are morally good.

These morally good actions are demonstrative of the renewal of your thought process.

You will be in a place where you're not always accusing somebody else, but taking personal responsibility for the things that happen to you in your life. You must learn to take personal responsibility for what happens to you in your life, because this allows you to begin to change.

Believers who spend time in God's word rather than accepting worldly ideas cultivate a transformed mind.

They don't look at the world the way everybody else looks at the world.

We must rise and dominate our circumstances, our feelings, our personal hang-ups, and turn our mindsets towards God, towards truth, and create a movement toward dominance over our feelings. We must tell our emotions, "I will not be sad. I will not be depressed. I will not be down. I will be up because the word of God says the truth shall set me

GOD CAN DELIVER

free." The word of God says all things will work together for good for those who love God who are called according to His purpose.

The word of God says that Jesus came to give life and that life more abundantly. God provides for our needs, and we need to look forward to His provision. We need to expect it.

CHAPTER 29

Dominated

When we immerse ourselves in God and His word, we become empowered in Christ rather than being dominated by the subtle wiles of the devil. We become personally responsible for the situations we find ourselves in. And as a result, we become personally responsible, with God's help and God's truth, for the victory we experience. It's an awesome thing. We know it's all God, we know it's all His power, and we know the only way we can have freedom and victory is through Him. But it takes purposeful willpower on our parts.

Christians operating in the proper spiritual perspectives will rise to dominate their circumstances rather than be dominated by them.

If a house is dirty, it doesn't get cleaned by you sitting around and complaining about the fact that it's dirty. It gets cleaned by you getting up and getting it done, by cleaning what's dirty. If your spiritual life is a mess and your physical and emotional life is a mess, sitting around complaining about it will not fix it. You need to rise up and ask God for help. Put your hand to work and change your situation.

You change your actions by changing your thoughts. You change your thoughts by putting the truth into your mind and thinking the way God would have you think.

The devil will not be able to pull you down when you put yourself in this position. You become actively working against him. You recognize his work and refuse to be subjected to him.

It will take a strong determination on your part. Start feeding your spirit with the proper diet of the word of God, get in contact with God through prayer, cut out the spiritual poison that you feed yourself with every day.

> ***You won't be able to win victory against the devil if you spend four hours a day feeding on the devil's slop through the television but you can't find ten minutes to feed on God's written word.***

If your doing this you must rent right now and turn back to the Lord.

Self-pity is a victim mentality that says "I deserve more"; this mindset is not going to help you or your family or the community you live in. Change happens when you finally accept God's truth as your own and you say, "I'm going to take that and I'm going to make it my own and I'm going to become something different than I am now through God's help. I'm going to overcome the circumstances that have held me down for my entire life. I'm going to be the person that God created me to be. I'm also going to become a blessing to the people that are around me. I'm going to preach this truth. I'm going to see the lost get saved and the captives set free."

> ***You can be that person. Remember, as a Christian, you should want to be like Jesus.***

You should want to be somebody who stands up boldly for the truth, but is also loving, caring, and compassionate.

DOMINATED

Every circumstance is different, and people have their own different stories. God made us all differently with our own strengths and weaknesses. However, in one way He made us all the same: with free will so that we can turn towards Him and praise Him. That is why I wrote this book – to help you, whatever your circumstances, recognize the way the enemy works in the world and learn to fight him for Christ.

CHAPTER 30

Two Dangers

After this manner, therefore pray you, Our Father which art in heaven, hallowed be thy name. Thy kingdom come, thy will be done on earth as it is in heaven. Give us this day our daily bread And forgive us our debts, as we forgive our debtors. Lead us not into temptation, but deliver us from the evil one, for thine is the kingdom and the power and the glory forever. Amen. (Matthew 6:9-13, KJV)

There's evil in this world; there is no doubt about that. God's word not only reveals that there is a source of evil, the evil one, but also that there is a need for deliverance or rescue. He says, "deliver us from the evil one." There is a need for rescue from the influence of the enemy. There is a force and a source of evil that would destroy your life, your family, and your personhood, and would destroy the nation you live in if given the chance. This one deceives entire nations.

In Revelation 20:2-3 we read:

And he laid hold on the dragon, that old serpent, which is the Devil, and Satan, and bound him a thousand years, And cast him into the bottomless pit, and shut him up, and set a seal upon him, that he should deceive the nations no more, till the thousand years should be fulfilled: and after that he must be loosed a little season. (KJV)

TWO DANGERS

Jesus died 2,000 years ago; therefore, Satan has been loosed from captivity for just over 1,000 years, according to this verse, to run to and fro, to deceive and manipulate the entire world.

I've got a short story I want to share with you. I had a friend of mine come from India for a visit. I picked him up in my old beat-up Ford truck with a wood bed on the back. He was fresh in from Northeast Nagaland, India. We went to the supermarket, and all he wanted to know was where the rice was. We went to the section where the rice was, and his eyes went big as saucers. There were 50 kinds of rice.

He said, "I just want the plain rice."

Even the poorest among us are wealthy. He walked out the door and he says, "How is everyone in America so wealthy?" At the time, I was a poor Bible college student with a $250 Ford Pickup Truck. He says, "In my country you live like a king."

The enemy would deceive the wealthiest and the poorest among us, making us think that the only way we can get anything is by taking it from someone else.

The enemy makes you think that there's no right and wrong, no absolutes.

It's a dangerous mindset, the mindset that I am owed something, that there is an evil being perpetrated upon me by people above me. The enemy has perpetrated this lie upon our culture. He has deceived our nation to where it is okay to even kill somebody else (such as through abortion) if you want too.

TWO DANGERS

As we look at the work of the evil one, we can see that the tactics and work of the evil one used in our country, the United States of America, are very specific.

There are two dangers that we need to be mindful of in every situation and circumstance of our lives.

1. We underestimate our enemy.
2. We overestimate our enemy.

One thing we certainly don't need to do is be giving the devil the traits of God. The devil is not God; he's subject to God and he is limited by God. We don't need to make him a god. He is not my God, I know that. He is the god of this world. But I'm not of this world.

And if you believe in Jesus Christ, you're not of this world, and the deivl not your God either.

There are those—even in the church—who deny that Satan is real and can influence the believer to do wrong. That is to *underestimate* our enemy. There are those who focus too much on Satan, seeing a demon behind every tree and blaming him for everything in their lives—even the bad choices that they themselves make—and that is *overestimating* our enemy.

CHAPTER 31

The Enemy's Abilities

We serve the one true God, the One to whom Satan himself is subject. What are Satan's goals, his abilities, his tactics, and his methods? This is information you need to know so you can live a life of victory over the evil one by not yielding to his influence.

1 Peter 5:8-9 says:

> *Be sober-minded; be watchful. Your adversary the devil prowls around like a roaring lion, seeking someone to devour. Resist him, firm in your faith, knowing that the same kinds of suffering are being experienced by your brotherhood throughout the world.*

Peter was writing to Christians when he wrote this. Be sober-minded; that means pay attention. The Greek word for "sober-minded" means to be prudently watchful and cautious in the face of danger or risk.

Consider the word "seeking."

The devil plots against your life, seeking whom he may devour, seeking whom he may destroy.

Peter was writing to Christians who were enduring severe persecution for their faith. In chapter one, he acknowledged that his readers "have been grieved by various trials." There were men who were putting to death Christians who remained faithful to Jesus. Peter realized that behind the men who were persecuting them, devouring them, there was

THE ENEMY'S ABILITIES

a spiritual reality. As Paul said, "we do not wrestle against flesh and blood, but against the rulers, against the authorities, against the cosmic powers over this present darkness, against the spiritual forces of evil in the heavenly places."

> **Peter was exhorting these believers to remain faithful to Christ even under the threats of persecution.**

Satan puts blinders on those who are outside of Christ. He wants to keep unbelievers from coming to Christ, and he most certainly wants to render you completely ineffective as a Christian. The devil wants to get you so wrapped up with your own little problems, that you do not care about the needs of others or find the time to talk to anybody about Jesus.

As we have already seen, Satan wants to **deceive** you.

> *...false Christ and false prophets will show great signs and wonders to deceive, if possible, even the elect. (Matthew 24:24, KJV)*

This time that you and I are living in is similar to what Jesus described at that time. There are many false teachers false prophets who are satanically motivated to deceive people—even those in the church. Their objective is not to bring hope, not to heal, not to save, but instead to deceive, if possible, even the elect.

Secondly, he wants to **hinder**. Look at 1 Thessalonians 2:18:

> *...we wanted to come to you—I, Paul, again and again—but Satan hindered us.*

To "hinder" means to stop, to obstruct, to impede or to detain. Paul was going about doing the work of Christ. Paul

THE ENEMY'S ABILITIES

wrote more of the New Testament than anybody else. Paul visited more missionary places than anyone else up to that point, winning more people to Christ than anyone up to that point. In his epistle to the church in Thessalonica, he wrote that he wanted to come to them, but Satan hindered him.

Now, there are a couple things we need to notice about this Scripture. First and foremost, we need to acknowledge that we are not perfect enough to keep Satan from hindering us.

I'm not the Apostle Paul. I think he definitely received more clarity from the Holy Spirit than I do. He definitely had more of the revelation of God, and he was one of the greatest missionaries that ever lived.

So, it's important to take note that one of the greatest missionaries that ever lived, said, "I wanted to come to you, but Satan hindered me."

If Satan can hinder a man of God such as the Apostle Paul, he can definitely hinder us.

How does this hindrance work in your life? The first thing we must understand about a hinderance is that it can only slow you down, not permanently stop you; that is, unless you allow it too.

Paul did end up making it to Thessalonica. Sure, he was hindered, but it did not prevent God from what he wanted to accomplish through his servant Paul.

Your enemy wants you to quit trying.

But if you keep hammering away, keep knocking on the door, keep beating it down, keep pushing forward, believe that

THE ENEMY'S ABILITIES

you will not be denied, you will not turn back, you will not take any less from this than what God has said that you can have, and 100% believe that the devil will not be able to stop you, you will succeed.

You will be victorious in the name of God.

CHAPTER 32

More about the Enemy's Tactics

As we have already seen, Satan has specific tactics that he employs to deceive and hinder. These tactics are **deceptive**, for he seeks to stay unnoticed. If he can keep you from identifying him, he succeeds.

Consider Acts 16:16-17:

> As we were going to the place of prayer, we were met by a slave girl who had a spirit of divination and brought her owners much gain by fortune-telling. She followed Paul and us, crying out, "These men are servants of the Most High God, who proclaim to you the way of salvation."

Would you like somebody following you around saying, "This is the servant of the most high God who proclaims the way of salvation"? Doesn't sound like much of a hindrance to me.

However, Paul didn't like it. She was a demon-possessed girl with a spirit of divination who was telling others about them.

> And this she kept doing for many days. Paul, having become greatly annoyed, turned and said to the spirit, "I command you in the name of Jesus Christ to come out of her." (Acts 16:18)

Paul was both annoyed and angry with what was happening. There were several reasons for this. The woman was demon-inspired, and Paul certainly did not want the

MORE ABOUT THE ENEMY'S TACTICS

people he was witnessing to thinking that he and she were working together.

Furthermore, the motivation for her doing this was greed. Luke reported that she "brought her owners much gain by fortune-telling." Paul did not want to contribute to such a base business as the men had made of her. Also, he wanted to deliver her from her wretched condition since she was a woman made in God's image who was been debased and was being destroyed by demonic power.

This incident is a good example of Satan's deceptive tactics. The second tactic is **ignorance**. In 2 Corinthians 2:11, we are told not to be ignorant:

> ...lest Satan should take advantage of us, for we are not ignorant of his devices.

To be ignorant is to be destitute of knowledge, uninstructed or uninformed. Unfortunately, millions of people who say they're Christian are not informed when it comes to the things of the enemy.

Now, the devil works in this ignorance. This is not a matter of needing more education in general. Sometimes education can be a hindrance, because people think they know more than God does.

> **When education is purely secular without the revelation of God, it is a work of ignorance about spiritual things that matter.**

The third tactic is **confusion**. Look at James 1:5-8:

> If any of you lacks wisdom, let him ask God, who gives generously to all without reproach,

MORE ABOUT THE ENEMY'S TACTICS

and it will be given him. But let him ask in faith, with no doubting, for the one who doubts is like a wave of the sea that is driven and tossed by the wind. For that person must not suppose that he will receive anything from the Lord; he is a double-minded man, unstable in all his ways.

James, a man of faith, didn't question it; he said wisdom would be given to him.

But let him ask in faith with no doubting for he who doubts is like a wave of the sea, driven and tossed by the wind for let, not that man suppose he will receive anything from the Lord. He is a double-minded man, unstable in all his ways.

The word that James used here is "dipsuchos", which literally means "two-souled". It means wavering, or having a divided interest. It describes the person who has two minds: one that is turned toward God desiring to please Him, but another that is turned toward the things of the world and his own fleshly desires. This person is in confusion, not knowing which way he should go.

If a person spends the majority of his time in worldly pursuits and thinking worldly thoughts, he will not be effective in serving the Lord.

It is with these methods of deception, ignorance, and confusion that the enemy can keep you from resisting him. If he can keep your will in limbo, not sure what to do, he can keep you defeated in your Christian walk.

CHAPTER 33

ight Him

Now, to fight Satan's methods, we must know the word of God.

Satan's methods always contradict the word of God.

Satan deceives lost people into thinking that they can enter heaven by being good enough. "Well, I'm better than the next guy down the street. I mean, he's cheating on his wife. I don't curse and yell and scream at all hours of the night at my family. I'm better than they are. I don't do drugs like so many other people."

However, you cannot get to heaven by being good enough. Every single person is a sinner who has fallen short of God's standard of holiness. The Apostle Paul quoted the Old Testament to establish this truth:

> *None is righteous, no, not one; no one understands; no one seeks for God. All have turned aside; together they have become worthless; no one does good, not even one. (Psalm 53:1-3)*

> *There is a way that seems right to a man but in the end, there is the way of death. You can't be good enough. (Proverbs 14:12, KJV)*

There's only one who was good enough, and His name is Jesus. Unless you receive the forgiveness He purchased on the cross, you will perish.

There are only two paths that humans can take; that is why Jesus exhorted sinners to enter in by the narrow gate that leads to heaven:

> *Enter by the narrow gate. For the gate is wide*
> *and the way is easy that leads to destruction,*
> *and those who enter by it are many.*
> *(Matthew 7:13)*

I heard someone say one time that you can go to heaven with the hypocrites or you can go to hell with them.

> *And when Jesus heard it, he said to*
> *them, "Those who are well have no need of a*
> *physician, but those who are sick. I came not to*
> *call the righteous, but sinners." (Mark 2:17)*

The church is nothing but a bunch of broken people who are saved by grace. That means when you get around God's people, you're around a bunch of imperfect people, me included. We are imperfect people because God has come to call sinners. He didn't come to call saints; He came to save sinners and make them saints.

It is through this process in our lives that we come together as the body of Christ. We study the word, and we learn what we need to learn. We love one another, and we care for one another, and we reach out to one another, and we help one another.

We are imperfect beings that try to imitate a perfect God.

And yeah, there's even a few hypocrites around, so what? That's just life. Hey, I might even be one of them every once in a while, and so might you. But when God reveals it to me, I'll repent, and ask Him to forgive me. And I hope you do too. We give each other grace and love. And that does a lot for hypocrisy.

> *And let us consider how to stir up one another to love and good works, not neglecting to meet together, as is the habit of some, but encouraging one another, and all the more as you see the day drawing near.*
> *(Hebrews 10:24-25)*

We are 2,000 years closer to the return of Christ than the day He left. And so every day that we are here, and with every week that passes by, it is so much more important that we find ourselves assembling together, where we can have support from one another.

It is tough to remain a faithful Christian outside of the fellowship of church.

You don't have to go to any church in particular, but be sure that you attend a church where the word of God is faithfully proclaimed.

CHAPTER 34

The Calling

The calling that God has put on a Christian believer is not to go out and live however you want. We believe fully and totally in the security of the believer, and we believe those that wholly believe in Christ will go to heaven.

However, what is a believer? A believer is someone who has truly repented of his sin and places his faith in Christ and follows after Christ.

A believer is somebody who not only talks the faith with their mouths but lives it out in their actions.

Christ has changed their hearts by giving them eternal life, and they now desire to live in obedience to Him. God has not called us to live in sin. God has called us to righteousness and holiness.

One of Satan's tactics against the church is to instigate disunity. That was why Paul reminded the Ephesians in chapter four of the importance of maintaining unity in the body:

> *I therefore, a prisoner for the Lord, urge you to walk in a manner worthy of the calling to which you have been called, with all humility and gentleness, with patience, bearing with one another in love, eager to maintain the unity of the Spirit in the bond of peace. (Ephesians 4:1-3)*

Another tactic of Satan in our day is trying to get church people to accept all things that are supernatural as if they are

THE CALLING

from God. All that is supernatural—or claims to be supernatural—is not necessarily from God. There are two sources for the supernatural, God and the devil.

Christians today need to be very discerning, because there are many false teachers and false prophets in the church. The Apostle John warned believers in 1 John 4:1:

> *Beloved, do not believe every spirit, but test the spirits to see whether they are from God, for many false prophets have gone out into the world.*

Now, not every supernatural event or supposed claim of a supernatural event is of God. There are supernatural events that take place for the sole purpose of deceiving those who believe. There are false prophets and false teachers, people who make themselves out to be Christians and make themselves out to be pastors, apostles, and prophets, but they are not. They are working for the enemy.

Look again at Jesus' words in Matthew 7:13-16:

> *Enter by the narrow gate. For the gate is wide and the way is easy that leads to destruction, and those who enter by it are many. For the gate is narrow and the way is hard that leads to life, and those who find it are few. Beware of false prophets, who come to you in sheep's clothing but inwardly are ravenous wolves. You will recognize them by their fruits. Are grapes gathered from thornbushes, or figs from thistles?*

THE CALLING

And what did Jesus also say? That a good tree does not bear bad fruit and a bad tree does not bear good fruit.

You will know them by their fruits.

Is there love? Is there joy? Is there peace? Is there long-suffering? Is there gentleness? Is there kindness? Is there humility? Is there fidelity to the word of God? Is there a meekness that flows forth from those who claim to be men of God? Check the fruit that they are producing to see if they are really servants of God.

Test the spirits to see if they are from God so you won't be one of those who are deceived. Jesus said the narrow gate is the way that leads to life, and there are few that find it.

CHAPTER 35

Jesus Came

Jesus came to set the captives free. This is the purpose for which Jesus Christ came to the earth.

Jesus came to set the captives free from the power of the devil.

Jesus came, for one reason: mankind was under the bondage of the enemy and His purpose was to break that bondage, to set those that were captives free.

Isaiah 61:1 says:

The Spirit of the Lord God is upon me, because the Lord has anointed me to bring good news to the poor; he has sent me to bind up the brokenhearted, to proclaim liberty to the captives, and the opening of the prison to those who are bound...

Jesus is the one who has come to set the captives free, to heal the brokenhearted. Have you ever been brokenhearted? Jesus came to heal your broken heart. Do you ever feel like you've been in bondage? Jesus came to set you free, to proclaim liberty to those who are captives. Have you ever felt bound? Jesus has come to open the prison that binds you.

Acts 10:38 says:

...how God anointed Jesus of Nazareth with the Holy Spirit and with power. He went about doing good and healing all who were oppressed by the devil, for God was with him.

JESUS CAME

There are at least 15 references directly commenting on Jesus casting out demons and setting people free from the oppression of the devil.

When Jesus Himself was tempted by the devil, He did specific things as we learn in Matthew 4:1-11:

> *Then Jesus was led up by the Spirit into the wilderness to be tempted by the devil. And after fasting forty days and forty nights, he was hungry. And the tempter came and said to him, "If you are the Son of God, command these stones to become loaves of bread." But he answered, "It is written, "'Man shall not live by bread alone, but by every word that comes from the mouth of God.'" Then the devil took him to the holy city and set him on the pinnacle of the temple and said to him, "If you are the Son of God, throw yourself down, for it is written, "'He will command his angels concerning you,' And "'On their hands they will bear you up, lest you strike your foot against a stone.'" Jesus said to him, "Again it is written, 'You shall not put the Lord your God to the test.'" Again, the devil took him to a very high mountain and showed him all the kingdoms of the world and their glory. And he said to him, "All these I will give you, if you will fall down and worship me." Then Jesus said to him, "Be gone, Satan! For it is written, "'You shall worship the Lord your God and him only shall you serve.'" Then the devil left him, and behold, angels came and were ministering to him.*

JESUS CAME

Let's dig a little deeper into how Jesus dealt with temptation from the devil.

CHAPTER 36

How Jesus Dealt with the Evil One

Then Jesus said to him, "Be gone, Satan! For it is written, "'You shall worship the Lord your God and him only shall you serve.'" Then the devil left him, and behold, angels came and were ministering to him. (Matthew 10-11)

Now in this story, we see specifically how Jesus dealt with the devil.

First, He quoted Scripture.

In response to Satan's temptation to turn stones into bread, Jesus quoted Deuteronomy 8:3. In response to Satan's temptation to cast Himself off the temple, Jesus quoted Deuteronomy 6:16. In response to Satan's temptation to give Him the kingdoms of the world before His crucifixion and resurrection when the Father would give Him all authority on earth and in heaven, Jesus responded with Deuteronomy 6:13:

*You shall fear the Lord your God
and serve Him alone.*

So He quoted Scripture. Now, there's only one possible way that you can utilize Scripture to resist Satan, and that's if you know the Scriptures.

The first thing that Jesus did when He came against the temptation of the enemy was to quote memorized Scripture.

HOW JESUS DEALT WITH THE EVIL ONE

Now, if you're not reading your Bible, you'll never memorize your Bible. If you're not putting the word of God into your mind, you'll never be able to remember the word of God when you face temptation. This is what Jesus did to overcome the enemy, overcome the evil one, to resist the devil when he was tempted.

Secondly, He applied truth in response to lies.

The antidote to Satan's lies is God's truth. Jesus said this in John 17:17:

Sanctify them in the truth; your word is truth.

Jesus said, "God's word is truth." He didn't say God's word conveys some idea that is true. He didn't say God's word might give someone a good idea about the way I should think about some things that might be true.

God's word is absolute truth.

We believe, as Jesus believed, that God's word is true. It is truth. So He quoted Scripture, He applied truth. Many believers doubt the veracity of the Old Testament. We have seen that Jesus quote the Old Testament as the infallible word of God in His encounter with Satan in the wilderness. We have seen that Jesus believed in the writings of Moses, and we see this again in John 3:14:

And as Moses lifted up the serpent in the wilderness, so must the Son of Man be lifted up...

You will be blessed when you take Jesus' attitude or position on the veracity of God's word and apply it to your life. By doing so, you will please your Heavenly Father. All you have to do is have faith that the Scriptures are true, and devote time to learning and memorizing them.

HOW JESUS DEALT WITH THE EVIL ONE

Our authority over the devil is the use of the word of God.

CHAPTER 37

Jesus' Tactics

Jesus did not engage in debate with demonic spirits. Notice what Mark reported about Jesus' dealings with demons in Mark 1:34:

And he healed many who were sick with various diseases, and cast out many demons. And he would not permit the demons to speak, because they knew him.

This tells us two things:

1. **He could cast them out.**
2. **He didn't want them to speak.**

He told them to be quiet. He did not allow the demons to speak. Jesus had absolute authority over the demonic realm. These beings are completely subject to His rule, and He did not engage in debate with liars. The devil is a liar and the father of it.

Jesus simply applied His authority. Look to Luke 4:41:

And demons also came out of many, crying, "You are the Son of God!" But he rebuked them and would not allow them to speak, because they knew that he was the Christ.

Now, a little side note here, do you realize how religious the devil and his demons are? They are religious beings. They know all of the religious terms and jargon. They know things of the Spirit. They know the word of God, and they are religious. And the only way you can tell the difference between

JESUS' TACTICS

them is by testing the spirits. What does the Bible say? The Bible says:

> *Whoever confesses that Jesus is the Son of God, God abides in him, and he in God. (1 John 4:15)*

Jesus commanded that they depart from a man with an unclean spirit. Look at Mark 1:23-26:

> *And immediately there was in their synagogue a man with an unclean spirit. And he cried out, "What have you to do with us, Jesus of Nazareth? Have you come to destroy us? I know who you are—the Holy One of God." But Jesus rebuked him, saying, "Be silent, and come out of him!" And the unclean spirit, convulsing him and crying out with a loud voice, came out of him.*

At Jesus' command, the unclean spirit cried out, and convulsed him greatly and came out of him. Miracles like this authenticated Jesus' claim to be the Son of God and Israel's Messiah.

CHAPTER 38

Jesus' Teachings

We will now consider what Jesus taught about Satan and demons.

First, He taught that power over the devil indicated the arrival of the kingdom of God. Look to Luke 11:20:

> *But if it is by the finger of God that I cast out demons, then the kingdom of God has come upon you.*

"By the finger of God" is a significant expression, for the Ten Commandments were written by the finger of God according to Exodus 31:18. Jesus' ability to cast out demons by the finger of God meant that He was who He claimed to be: the Son of God and Israel's Messiah. They were telling him, "You cast out demons by Beelzebub the prince of demons." But Jesus said, "I cast out demons by the finger of God, and if I cast out demons by the finger of God then the kingdom of God has come upon you."

Now, what is a kingdom? A kingdom is a place where one rules, a place where a king has dominion. When Jesus expresses dominance over the devil, then the kingdom of God has arrived because the dominion, power, and authority of God is ruling and reigning.

The second thing Jesus taught is that spiritual power can be gained and applied against evil spirits. See Matthew 17:19-20:

> *Then the disciples came to Jesus privately and said, "Why could we not cast it out?" He said to them, "Because of your little faith. For truly, I*

JESUS' TEACHINGS

say to you, if you have faith like a grain of mustard seed, you will say to this mountain, 'Move from here to there,' and it will move, and nothing will be impossible for you."

In Matthew 17, a man has a son, and they called him a lunatic. The disciples came to Jesus privately, asking, "Why could we not cast it out?" Now this young boy was possessed by a devil that was throwing him in the water, trying to kill him, throwing him in the fire trying to kill him, trying to hurt him, trying to harm him. So, the man brings the boy to the disciples, and the disciples can't do anything about it. So the man comes to Jesus and Jesus takes care of business. And then the disciples come back to Him and say, why couldn't we do it? Jesus said simply this because of your unbelief because you don't believe you can.

if you have faith like a grain of mustard seed, you will say to this mountain, 'Move from here to there,' and it will move, and nothing will be impossible for you.

There is a spiritual power that can be gained by the child of God and applied against the evil spirits.

But it is a matter of faith, no different from when you got saved. It is a matter of faith. Jesus said the disciples can't do it because of their unbelief.

There has to come a point in time when you move forward, and you move into this truth, where you will be able to cast out demons just like Jesus did. It'll happen because you start believing the Bible to be true.

JESUS' TEACHINGS

Power over demons is achieved in the same way Jesus did it in the wilderness: by using the word of God.

Matthew 17:21 tells us two things. First, that there are varying degrees of demonic power. Okay, this particular kind needs to be taken out by prayer and fasting. The second thing there is a greater level of power that can be attained. It's just not free. It just doesn't just waft over to you when you become a believer. Rather, it is achieved by correct action. Jesus says it is achieved by prayer and fasting. And we know that Jesus did both of these on a regular basis.

Jesus would remove himself into the wilderness to pray. They would look around and He would be gone. And they were like, where is He? He was off on His own, praying. He did it in the Garden of Gethsemane before He went to the cross. We know He fasted at least one time for 40 days.

Fasting and prayer is a way for the believer to take the time to devote all his attention to God, seeking to commit his heart to the Lord and trust Him for help in whatever the believer is facing in life.

What is necessary for the believer today to resist demonic influence? The Bible is clear: it is the believer's trust in the word of God. The believer must believe God's word and use it to defeat the temptations of the enemy. Now all who have faith have the same power over evil, but many people don't understand this or utilize it.

Mark 16:17 says:

JESUS' TEACHINGS

And these signs will accompany those who believe: in my name they will cast out demons; they will speak in new tongues...

He didn't say the signs will follow those who have doubt, or those who walk in unbelief, or those who believe half of what Jesus said, but those who believe in the name of Jesus will cast out demons.

These signs will follow those who have faith in Jesus' name; they will cast out demons.

I don't know a lot of Christian people that do that. I just don't. And yet, it's the first thing that Jesus said would happen to those who believe in Him would be doing. This is a sign that would follow those who believe. Secondly, they will speak with new tongues.

And these signs will accompany those who believe: in my name they will cast out demons; they will speak in new tongues...

I looked up the word for "tongues"; it's **glossa**. It means a language not naturally acquired. So the verse simply says this: those who believe will speak in a language they did not learn. We saw that in the New Testament.

You can look at it in the book of Acts when people started speaking in tongues and everybody else started hearing what they had to say in their own language. Three thousand people came to know Christ that same day.

CHAPTER 39

His Kingdom

The kingdom of God is righteousness, peace and joy in the Holy Spirit.

What is the kingdom of God? The kingdom of God is the dominion of Jesus Christ. Following the resurrection, the Father entrusted Jesus with all authority in heaven and on earth. Jesus is now the sovereign ruler over heaven and earth.

When Jesus came to earth, the inauguration of His kingdom had arrived. Remember, Jesus said, "If I cast out demons by the finger of God, then the kingdom of God has come upon you."

God's children demonstrate that they are living by kingdom principles by living right, having peace which flows from inside, and feeling a joy unstoppable.

Who needs that? We all need that; we all need righteousness, the ability to live right. We all need peace in our hearts because we are living in a fallen world.

If I live in God, then I believe the word of God, and I act on the word of God as I take away my doubt and fear. I place my faith in the truth of God's word.

When you believe every word of the Bible, living by its truth, you will experience the peace of God even in the most difficult circumstances of your life.

You can look around you and see the suffering, trials, and wickedness that abound, yet if you are in Christ you will

HIS KINGDOM

experience the wonder of righteousness and peace and joy in the Holy Spirit.

CHAPTER 40

Power, Right, and Authority

Jesus said, You shall know the truth, and the truth will make you free. (John 8:32, KJV)

He expects those of us who know that truth to operate according to the truth.

The gospel message will reach the world around us only when it's manifested through us, in our honest and sincere relationship with God.

There are three powers of wills in this world: God, the devil, and man. God is love, He is good, He is creative, He is positive. The devil is hate, he is evil, he is destructive, and he is negative. Man is a neutral force. And by choice of will, man serves God, or by no choice at all, man serves evil.

Look what Paul wrote in Romans 3:12-18:

All have turned aside; together they have become worthless; no one does good, not even one." "Their throat is an open grave; they use their tongues to deceive." "The venom of asps is under their lips." "Their mouth is full of curses and bitterness." "Their feet are swift to shed blood; in their paths are ruin and misery, and the way of peace they have not known." "There is no fear of God before their eyes."

That is how it is. That is the biblical revelation that we have. By choice, we serve God, or by no choice, we serve evil.

POWER, RIGHT, AND AUTHORITY

We have an obligation to serve the Almighty God. You and I as believers have the right, the power, the authority to overcome the evil one.

Jesus operated in this authority. He had the power to teach, as we see in Matthew 7:28 and 29:

> *And when Jesus finished these sayings, the crowds were astonished at his teaching, for he was teaching them as one who had authority, and not as their scribes.*

He had power in His words to forgive:

> *...but you may know the Son of Man has power on earth to forgive sins. He said to the paralytic, I say to you, arise, take up your bed, and go to your house. And immediately he arose and took up the bed and went out in the presence of them all. (Mark 2:10-12, KJV)*

If you will take the Bible for exactly for what it says, as the revealed inspired, inerrant word of God, and you set yourself on that with all you have, and put all your eggs in that basket, you will not be disappointed. But if you take part of the word of God, and think in your heart, "I like this part, but I don't like that part," then you'll only be half blessed.

Hopefully, you're the Christian that has all his eggs in one basket. You believe the written word of God, every word that the Bible says. Then, when you're standing on the beach and the storm surges with all the blessings of God, just let it overtake you. When you believe that the Bible is 100% inerrant, that Jesus really did say to the paralyzed man, "Rise

POWER, RIGHT, AND AUTHORITY

and walk," and he really did take up his bed and walk away, then you will be blessed.

What God has asked us to do is to be obedient to Him and to keep His commandments.

He is not asking you to do anything that He did not ask Jesus to do. Jesus had the right and the power to not go to the cross. But He said specifically, "This command I have received from My Father." He did what God told Him to do.

Jesus had the power over all flesh. Look to the book of John 17:1-2:

> *When Jesus had spoken these words, he lifted up his eyes to heaven, and said, "Father, the hour has come; glorify your Son that the Son may glorify you, since you have given him authority over all flesh, to give eternal life to all whom you have given him.*

Do you wonder what eternal life is? Listen to Jesus. This is eternal life: that you may know the only true God and Jesus Christ, the One whom God has sent. What has God given us to do but this, that people may know God and Jesus Christ as their Savior?

This is eternal life: that you know God personally, that you come to Christ and embrace what He has done for you. This is eternal life.

CHAPTER 41

hrist Has Power

Jesus said that He had the power to give eternal life to everyone that the Father had given to Him. He had the power to heal. He had power over unclean spirits.

> *And they were all amazed and said to one another, "What is this word? For with authority and power he commands the unclean spirits, and they come out!"*

He had power over angels, authorities, and powers. Look at 1 Peter 3:22:

> *...who has gone into heaven and is at the right hand of God, with angels, authorities, and powers having been subjected to him.*

All rulers, all powers, all angels and authorities are subject to Jesus. He has that kind of power.

Jesus' authority over all creation is evidence that He is truly the Son of God and worthy of the believer's worship and obedience.

Jesus delegates this power and this authority to those who believe.

Now, the word "delegate" means to entrust or to commit; to deliver to another's care and exercise; to delegate authority or power to an envoy, representative, or a judge.

Jesus has delegated the authority that He has over the flesh. He has delegated the power that He has over unclean spirits. He has delegated the power that He has to heal. He has delegated the power He has over all thrones and dominions and authorities.

First, He delegated it to the disciples in Luke 9:1-2. He called the disciples together, He gave them power and authority over all demons, and the power to cure diseases. Then He sent them to preach the kingdom of God and to heal the sick.

The conferring of that authority gave them special status. And they were special. Look at what Luke wrote in Acts 5:12a:

Now many signs and wonders were regularly done among the people by the hands of the apostles.

And again in Matthew 10:1:

And he called to him his twelve disciples and gave them authority over unclean spirits, to cast them out, and to heal every disease and every affliction.

So here we have the delegated authority and power of Jesus given to the disciples.

He also gave it to many more.

In Luke 10:1 –

After this the Lord appointed seventy-two others and sent them on ahead of him, two by two, into every town and place where he himself was about to go.

And in verses 17-20:

HRIST HAS POWER

The seventy-two returned with joy, saying, "Lord, even the demons are subject to us in your name!" And he said to them, "I saw Satan fall like lightning from heaven. Behold, I have given you authority to tread on serpents and scorpions, and over all the power of the enemy, and nothing shall hurt you. Nevertheless, do not rejoice in this, that the spirits are subject to you, but rejoice that your names are written in heaven."

In John 14:9-14, Jesus promised that all believers will do His *works* and then that all believers will do *greater works*.

Jesus said to him, "Have I been with you so long, and you still do not know me, Philip? Whoever has seen me has seen the Father. How can you say, 'Show us the Father'? Do you not believe that I am in the Father and the Father is in me? The words that I say to you I do not speak on my own authority, but the Father who dwells in me does his works. Believe me that I am in the Father and the Father is in me, or else believe on account of the works themselves. Truly, truly, I say to you, whoever believes in me will also do the works that I do; and greater works than these will he do, because I am going to the Father. Whatever you ask in my name, this I will do, that the Father may be glorified in the Son. If you ask me anything in my name, I will do it."

The New Testament epistles where miracles are mentioned clearly state they are a gift that some Christians have and some do not. For example, in 1 Corinthians 12, Paul says:

> *To each is given the manifestation of the Spirit for the common good. For to one is given through the Spirit the utterance of wisdom, and to another the utterance of knowledge according to the same Spirit, to another faith by the same Spirit, to another gifts of healing by the one Spirit, to another the working of miracles, to another prophecy, to another the ability to distinguish between spirits, to another various kinds of tongues, to another the interpretation of tongues... Are all apostles? Are all prophets? Are all teachers? Do all work miracles? Do all possess gifts of healing? Do all speak with tongues? Do all interpret? But earnestly desire the higher gifts. (1 Corinthians 12:7-10, 29-31)*

If Jesus did not mean that all believers will do miracles like he did, what did he mean when he said, "Whoever believes in me will also do the works that I do"?

First, notice the connection between verse 11 and verse 12.

> *Believe me that I am in the Father and the Father is in me, or else believe on account of the works themselves. Truly, truly, I say to you, whoever believes in me will also do the works that I do; and greater works than these will he do, because I am going to the Father.*

The word "believe" and "works" occur together in verse 11 just like they come together in verse 12. Jesus' works are designed to help people believe.

His challenge was that if his verbal testimony was leaving doubts in people's mind about who he was, look at the works. Let the works join with the words and lead you to faith. That's what verse 11 says.

Then verse 12 follows:

"Truly, truly, I say to you, whoever believes in me will also do the works that I do."

Now put verse 11 and 12 together and let the function of the works be the same in both verses. Jesus' works function to lead people to faith in Christ. When you come to believe in Christ, He will work in you (like a vine works in a branch, John 15:1–7), and your works, like Jesus' works, will lead people to faith.

So the connection between verses 11 and 12 goes like this: "Believe in me on account of my works — let my works lead you to faith (verse 11), because whoever believes in me (verse 12) will also do works that lead people to believe in me."

So whatever the specific works are that Jesus had in mind, what defines them is that *they are pointers to Jesus which help people believe in Him.* They are a witness along with Jesus' gospel message that leads people to faith. That's what His works do, and He is saying that's what <u>all believers'</u> works will do.

CHRIST HAS POWER

If you are a believer in Jesus, that's what your life is—a living testimony of a life transformed by the gospel. Your works, your life are a display of the trustworthiness of Jesus.

Christians are defined by works or a life that is lived by faith in Jesus and point to the glory of Jesus.

What are the "greater works" that you will do—all of you? You will receive the Holy Spirit as the Spirit of the crucified and risen Christ. Before the resurrection of Jesus, nobody in the history of the world had ever experienced that!

In the power of that absolutely new experience — the indwelling of the crucified and risen Christ — your works of love and your message of life in union with Christ will point people to the glory of the risen Son of God, and you will be the instrument of their forgiveness on the basis of the finished work of Christ (John 20:23).

This will be new. This will be greater than Jesus' earthly miracles, because this is what He came to accomplish by His death and resurrection.

CHAPTER 42

God Gave Us His Name

Christ gave us the power of attorney to use His name.

What is the power of attorney? It is the right to act in the name of or on behalf of another in the same power and authority as if the person acted or was present. All believers have the legal and redemptive right to use the name of Jesus over the demonic. That's powerful. That probably moves you into a realm that you've not been before. That moves you into a place of power that you've not had before.

Let's look at some Scriptures that express the Christians' power of attorney to use Jesus' name.

Matthew 18:19-20:

Again I say to you, if two of you agree on earth about anything they ask, it will be done for them by my Father in heaven. For where two or three are gathered in my name, there am I among them."

I'll tell you what, this particular truth right here is one of those that have got to be too good to be true but it's not, because we believe every word that's written in the Bible.

In Mark 16 –

And these signs will accompany those who believe: in my name they will cast out demons; they will speak in new tongues; they will pick up serpents with their hands; and if they drink any deadly poison, it will not hurt them; they will

GOD GAVE US HIS NAME

*lay their hands on the sick, and they will
recover. (Mark 16:17-18)*

Now that's protection, isn't it? That's saying those who believe have divine protection on our lives. If you happen to drink something deadly and you don't know that it was rat poison for dinner, by mistake, something crazy like that, you can believe that God will take care of you. He's got that power. And He shares/delegates it to those who believe in His name.

Now, I am NOT telling you to go out and eat rat poison for dinner. No. *Thou shalt not tempt the Lord thy God.* But He will look out for you in difficult circumstances.

I wonder how many accidents you should have had, but God kept you out of them. I can name a bunch of them myself. How many can you recall? You can guarantee there's at least a few, and probably even many you don't know about, because God looked out for you. It's protection. I love that!

One of the ways in which Jesus protects us is by warning us through the guidance of the Holy Spirit. In John 16:13, Jesus states:

*When the Spirit of truth comes, he will guide you
into all the truth, for he will not speak on his
own authority, but whatever he hears he will
speak, and he will declare to you the
things that are to come.*

Are you a part of a congregation that is doing what God has asked us to do in the face of much opposition, including opposition from the enemy, opposition from those who don't love God, and opposition from all the forces of the evil one?

GOD GAVE US HIS NAME

I personally will never stop. I will do what God has asked me to do.

And you my friend, if you believe and truly love God, should be obedient to what God has asked you to do. Only then can you walk with peace, and walk in the power of God in your life. Then, you too can overcome the evil one.

CHAPTER 43

Power to Witness

God gives special power to believers for the extraordinary challenges of an expanding witness to Christ. This was the point that Jesus made in Acts 1:8:

But you will receive power when the Holy Spirit has come upon you, and you will be my witnesses in Jerusalem and in all Judea and Samaria, and to the end of the earth.

This power Christ promised is essential for the challenges of an ever-expanding witness of the gospel to lost people for the glory of Christ. Jesus was clear in making this connection when he said, "and you shall be my witnesses in Jerusalem and in all Judea and Samaria and to the end of the earth."

We see this power that came upon the church and its messengers again and again in the early church for the special challenges of witnessing for Christ.

In the book of acts, we see Peter, filled with the Holy Spirit, spoke to the rulers of the people. And they saw the boldness with which he spoke.

And when they had prayed, the place in which they were gathered together was shaken and they were all filled with the Spirit and spoke the word of God with boldness. (Acts 4:31)

In Acts 6:5-10: Stephen was full of the Holy Spirit and faith and the Jews could not withstand the wisdom with which he spoke.

POWER TO WITNESS

In Acts 11:24, Barnabas was full of the Holy Spirit and faith, and a large company was added to the Lord.

But Saul, who was also called Paul, filled with the Holy Spirit, looked intently at him...
(Acts 13:9)

Luke 4:14 says that Jesus returned from the wilderness full of the Holy Spirit. Jesus withstood the devil with power in the wilderness, but how?

Every time He was attacked, He answered, "It is written." He quoted Scripture. Jesus was full of the Spirit because He was full of the word of God.

The power that stopped Satan in his tracks was the word of God.

The power that the New Testament promises believers everywhere is the Holy Spirit's God-breathed word of God.

CHAPTER 44

The Unbeliever

If you don't know Christ, you desperately need to realize that you stand before God as guilty of breaking His moral law. Your sins are "earning wages" that will bring condemnation on the day that Jesus mankind.

Paul said, "For the wages of sin is death, but the free gift of God is eternal life in Christ Jesus our Lord."

Christ paid the debt of your sin on the cross, and you need to turn from your sins and place your trust in Christ.

Suppose you were on a plane that was about to crash, and the stewardess said, "If you put on this parachute and jump, you will be saved from dying." You would put your trust in that parachute rather than go down in a flaming crash. In the same way, the Bible tells us that if we put our trust in Jesus Christ, we will be given Jesus' righteousness and pardoned from our sins. The Apostle Paul gave every believer this assurance in Romans 8:1:

There is therefore now no condemnation for those who are in Christ Jesus.

If you are not born again, Jesus said you must be born again. The Spirit of God must give life to you and make you a new creation in Christ Jesus. You have no defense against the enemy outside of Jesus Christ.

...but God shows his love for us in that while we were still sinners, Christ died for us.
(Romans 5:8)

THE UNBELIEVER

*For the wages of sin is death, but the free gift of
God is eternal life in Christ Jesus our Lord.
(Romans 6:23)*

If you do not know Jesus Christ, you have no life in Him. Your destination is hell. And there is only one possible way that you can go to heaven and that is through believing in Him. It is the only hope.

If you need to find God, pray to Him. If you need help, you can pray words like these:

> *God, I admit that I am a sinner. I have broken Your holy law again and again and I am worthy of Your judgment. I now believe the Lord Jesus Christ died for my sins on that cross and was raised so that I could be forgiven of all my sins and receive the righteousness of Christ. I receive and confess Jesus as my personal Savior.*

Now, you can say Amen, which simply means "I believe." If you prayed that prayer today, and you meant it from your heart, God has promised that whoever truly places his trust in Christ will be saved. Your position has gone from the kingdom of darkness into His marvelous light. And you can know that your destination is not hell, but heaven.

Romans 10:9-10 says if you've believed and then confessed, Jesus is your Savior today.

> *if you confess with your mouth that Jesus is
> Lord and believe in your heart that God raised
> him from the dead, you will be saved. For with
> the heart one believes and is justified, and with
> the mouth one confesses and is saved.*

THE UNBELIEVER

Confession of Christ before others is important, and Paul emphasizes that in verse nine. In verse 10, he reminded the Romans of the order of salvation: one believes and is justified. That means that he is declared righteous before God on the basis of Jesus' death. Then the person confesses before others.

A "faith" that does not have the vital force to produce confession before others is not saving faith.

James made this point when he wrote, "Even the demons believe—and shudder!" Saving faith is not just an intellectual acknowledgment of Jesus, but is a heart trust in the person and work of Jesus Christ as Savior.

CHAPTER 45

The Whole Armor of God

The Apostle Paul gave believers this exhortation about our spiritual enemy:

Finally, be strong in the Lord and in the strength of his might. Put on the whole armor of God that you may be able to stand against the schemes of the devil. For we do not wrestle against flesh and blood, but against the rulers, against the authorities, against the cosmic powers over this present darkness, against the spiritual forces of evil in the heavenly places. Therefore take up the whole armor of God that you may be able to withstand in the evil day, and having done all, to stand firm. (Ephesians 6:10-13)

As he made clear, this isn't a battle against people of flesh and blood. This is a spiritual battle. It is a battle against the rulers, against the authorities, against the cosmic powers over this present darkness, against the spiritual forces of evil in the heavenly places..

Because it is a spiritual battle, the armor that God gives us is spiritual armor to fight a spiritual enemy in a spiritual battle.

A friend once asked the following questions: "Do you suppose it was God that made me a drug addict? Do you suppose it was God that made me hurt people? Do you suppose it was God that took me away from my family? Do you suppose it was God that didn't have me call my mom for

THE WHOLE ARMOR OF GOD

about five years in a row? I suppose it was God that alienated me from any source of strength or hope, or power? I suppose it was God that had me move into a drug addict's house? Spend all my money on drugs? I suppose it was God that did that."

The answer is no. No, it wasn't God that did that. That was the scheming of the devil to tempt like that.

God desires that all people would be saved. If you do not know God, you should repent today and turn to Christ. If you are a believer, you should desire to share the good news of the gospel with others that they might be saved.

To stand for Christ and against the schemes of the devil, take up the whole armor of God. Have you put on the armor of God?

Take up the whole armor of God. Put on the entire armor of God.

CHAPTER 46

Six Parts

There are six parts of the armor. Have you put every piece on?

If you can't tell me what it means to be saved, you don't have on the **helmet of salvation**.

If you can't tell me what it means to be righteous, you don't have on the **breastplate of righteousness**.

If you are not learning the word of God, you don't have on the **belt of truth**.

If you live in conflict, consistent, constant conflict with other human beings, you don't walk with your **feet shod with the preparation of the gospel of peace**.

And if you can't answer the problems in your life with Scripture, you've not put on the **sword of the Spirit**, which is the word of God.

If your faith in Christ is shaken, then you are not carrying **the shield of faith**.

> ***Whatever piece you don't have, you need to identify it. Then you need to begin to work at putting it on.***

Finally, be strong in the Lord and in the strength of his might. Put on the whole armor of God, that you may be able to stand against the schemes of the devil. For we do not wrestle against flesh and blood, but against the rulers, against the authorities, against the cosmic powers over this present darkness, against the

SIX PARTS

spiritual forces of evil in the heavenly places. Therefore take up the whole armor of God, that you may be able to withstand in the evil day, and having done all, to stand firm. Stand therefore, having fastened on the belt of truth, and having put on the breastplate of righteousness, and, as shoes for your feet, having put on the readiness given by the gospel of peace. In all circumstances take up the shield of faith, with which you can extinguish all the flaming darts of the evil one; and take the helmet of salvation, and the sword of the Spirit, which is the word of God, praying at all times in the Spirit, with all prayer and supplication. To that end, keep alert with all perseverance, making supplication for all the saints...
(Ephesians 6:10-18)

These six items which constitute the complete armor of God are: truth, righteousness, peace, faith, salvation, and the word of God.

CHAPTER 47

Truth

*Finally, be strong in the Lord and in the strength of his might. Put on the whole armor of God, that you may be able to stand against the schemes of the devil. For we do not wrestle against flesh and blood, but against the rulers, against the authorities, against the cosmic powers over this present darkness, against the spiritual forces of evil in the heavenly places. Therefore take up the whole armor of God, that you may be able to withstand in the evil day, and having done all, to stand firm. Stand therefore, having fastened on the belt of truth, and having put on the breastplate of righteousness, and, as shoes for your feet, having put on the readiness given by the gospel of peace. In all circumstances take up the shield of faith, with which you can extinguish all the flaming darts of the evil one; and take the helmet of salvation, and the sword of the Spirit, which is the word of God, praying at all times in the Spirit, with all prayer and supplication. To that end, keep alert with all perseverance, making supplication for all the saints, and also for me, that words may be given to me in opening my mouth boldly to proclaim the mystery of the gospel, for which I am an ambassador in chains, that I may declare it boldly, as I ought to speak.
(Ephesians 6:10-20)*

TRUTH

Have you put on the belt of truth in your life? Do you live according to the truth? Look to Ephesians 6:14a:

Stand therefore, having fastened on the belt of truth...

What is truth? Truth is what is gleaned from a thorough study of the Scripture.

It is not just knowledge of Scriptural truth, but the truth that the believer has made his own that is in harmony with the objective truth found in the gospel.

It is now the truth that the believer not only believes but lives by.

CHAPTER 48

Righteousness

Stand therefore, having fastened on the belt of truth, and having put on the breastplate of righteousness... (Ephesians 6:14)

The breastplate of righteousness is living with moral integrity before God and others. God has called us to live righteously. The believer who lives a righteous life is not fearful of the accusations of the enemy. His heart is clean before God.

Paul wrote this in 1 Thessalonians 4:7:

For God has not called us for impurity, but in holiness.

In Romans 6:13, the apostle urged believers with this admonition:

Do not present your members to sin as instruments for unrighteousness, but present yourselves to God as those who have been brought from death to life, and your members to God as instruments for righteousness.

God has called us to holiness and if you will put on the armor, including the breastplate of righteousness, then you will be guarded against the enemy's attacks.

To be a believer is to have faith in Christ, fellowship with Christ, and follow after Christ.

RIGHTEOUSNESS

To follow Christ and live righteously is a call to a new life, a new way of living. It's a call to God's way and it's not easy. It will affect your life.

CHAPTER 49

Peace

...and, as shoes for your feet, having put on the readiness given by the gospel of peace.
(Ephesians 6:15)

The caligae, or sandals of the Roman soldiers, were heavy-soled shoes studded with hobnails to give a secure foothold.

The believer also needs sure footing in life, and that is supplied by the gospel of peace.

God gives us peace through Jesus Christ.

Romans 5:1 says this:

Therefore, since we have been justified by faith, we[a] have peace with God through our Lord Jesus Christ.

That peace surpasses all understanding, according to Philippians 4:7:

And the peace of God, which surpasses all understanding, will guard your hearts and your minds in Christ Jesus.

Living in peace follows God's gift of peace in salvation; it is not the requirement to receive it.

So then let us pursue what makes for peace and for mutual upbuilding. (Romans 14:9)

PEACE

It is the peace of God we receive in the gospel that grounds us in the battle against the enemy.

Don't think more highly of yourself than you want to think of others. Be willing to take offense.

Always think others have good motives until you are proven otherwise; that's how you overcome the evil one.

CHAPTER 50

Faith

In Ephesians 6:16, the apostle exhorts believers to always have the shield of faith at hand.

In all circumstances take up the shield of faith, with which you can extinguish all the flaming darts of the evil one...

The shield of faith means taking God at His word by believing His promises, despite the circumstances in your life.

Faith is a gift from God, according to Ephesians 2:8:

For by grace you have been saved through faith. And this is not your own doing; it is the gift of God.

You can quit smoking marijuana if you believe God has the power to deliver you, and you can overcome drunkenness if you believe.

If you believe in God's help, you can be good to people, and you can move out into the world and become a force for Almighty God.

CHAPTER 51

Salvation

For the next piece of armor, Ephesians 6:17a says to:

...and take the helmet of salvation...

Salvation here is what makes up our "state of salvation", accomplished by Jesus' atonement and received by grace—received in earnest now, realized in perfection in heaven.

> **God has redeemed you by paying the price for your sin through His death on the cross.**

There is no salvation in any other form, for there is no other name under heaven given among men by which we must be saved. That name is Jesus.

Romans 6:23 reminds us that salvation is from the wages that our sins have accrued:

For the wages of sin is death, but the gift of God is eternal life through Jesus Christ our Lord.

That's powerful.

Salvation is threefold. First, you have freedom from the just **penalty** of sin.

Then, you have freedom from the **power** of sin in your life. The believer is no longer a slave of sin.

Finally, you will have freedom from the **presence** of sin when you are in heaven with God.

SALVATION

The Apostle John wrote that the one who has placed his trust in Christ can "know" that he is saved—that he possesses eternal life:

> *I write these things to you who believe in the name of the Son of God, that you may know that you have eternal life. (1 John 5:13)*

This knowledge is a protection for the believer's heart when he is assaulted by the accusations of the enemy!

CHAPTER 52

God's Word

Last, but not least, is the sword of the Spirit, which is the word of God.

> ...and the sword of the Spirit, which is the word of God... (Ephesians 6:17b)

It's the only offensive weapon in the spiritual arsenal that God provides you. Everything else is a defensive weapon.

The word of God is different; it's an offensive weapon.

The glorious gospel message of Christ, wherever it is proclaimed, is able to put to shame *and* to fight the powers of evil.

The Bible is God's word to all men. We believe it was written by human authors under the guidance of the Holy Spirit. It is truth without any mixture of error. The words of the Lord are pure words like silver tried in a furnace of earth.

Psalm 119:160 makes this declaration about God's word:

> *The sum of your word is truth, and every one of your righteous rules endures forever.*

All of Scripture is without any mixture of error. God has given to us everything we need for life and godliness in His word.

The Christian's armor—the belt of truth, the breastplate of righteousness, the sandals for your feet, the shield of faith, the helmet of salvation, and the sword of the

GOD'S WORD

Spirit—should be put on and applied to the life of every child of God.

> ***These truths address every area of the enemy's spiritual attacks against you. The believer equipped with God's complete armor will not be defeated.***

You and I should move forward and be the aggressor in this spiritual battle that we fight. We should have our armor on and, taking the sword of the Spirit, can proclaim the gospel to those who are still in their sins. We should do this because we don't want anybody to die and go to hell without hearing the good news of what Jesus Christ has done for them.

CHAPTER 53

The Ultimate End—Victory of the Saints

The ultimate end of our war against the evil one is the victory of the saints. This is a wonderful thing to consider.

When things are getting tough and life seems full of trials, it is a comfort to the soul to bring to mind God's promise to the saints:

Whoever believes in the Son has eternal life.

While many people today believe there is nothing after death, but that life ends when our physical bodies die, Jesus gave us hope for life eternal. He proved the reality of life after death by His resurrection.

Human existence does not just take place on the physical plane; we are both material beings and spiritual beings.

We shall either spend eternity with God or we shall be cast into eternal torment. While we are here on this earth, we face many obstacles, one of them being the attacks of the enemy, Satan.

What we have learned from Ephesians 6 is that God has provided for our defense.

Resist the devil and he will flee from you. The Bible says this is so.

THE ULTIMATE END—VICTORY OF THE SAINTS

I like to talk about what will be. When I don't think I'm going to make it through another day, I like to talk about where the devil is going.

When the devil gets me down, I like to tell the devil where he's going. I say to the devil, "Devil, you're going to hell, but I'm not. You're going to be bound in the lake of fire for a thousand years, but I'm not. You're going to sit under the judgment of Almighty God, but I'm not. You are cursed, but I'm not".

God speaks truth through His word. He has given us a handbook of the past, the present, and the future.

The past includes the time of creation and the first sin and moving all the way to the present times between the first and second coming of Jesus Christ. The future where there will be a new heaven and a new earth and the former things will pass away when Christ comes again.

It is good to know where we are.

When we know in time where we are, we know what is expected of us, and how we will be judged by God.

It's a good thing to know what the expectations are for your life. If you don't know the expectations that God puts on your life, you're not possibly going to be able to fulfill them.

This is not a game that we want to play hit and miss with. Maybe I'll be good enough, maybe I won't. That's not going to cut it. You need to know what is expected of you. And then you can go about fulfilling that expectation.

THE ULTIMATE END—VICTORY OF THE SAINTS

In the next few chapters, we will discover where we are in the biblical timeline and what the future has in store for all of us. Also, we will learn what the future holds for the evil one so that you may overcome him as he attacks at will.

CHAPTER 54

The Times

Now, in what time do we live?

At this very moment that we find ourselves, we are close to the end times. We have the dispensation of grace, a dispensation that is a period when God deals with man under a specific set of guidelines or principles. That's what a dispensation is – a period when God deals with man under a certain set of principles or guidelines.

This is the dispensation of grace. That is the unmerited favor of God brought to us by faith in Jesus Christ.

This is a period when what God expects from us is to believe in the Lord Jesus Christ. And by that belief, faith in the Lord Jesus Christ, we have eternal life, and all that goes along with it. That is the dispensation of grace.

Grace came with Jesus in John 1:17 –

For the law was given through Moses; grace and truth came through Jesus Christ.

Jesus said in John 8:32 –

...and you will know the truth, and the truth will set you free.

Free from what? That is the question that I ask and the question is answered with this: you will be free from the curse of the law.

Look to Romans 8:2 –

THE TIMES

For the law of the Spirit of life has set you free in Christ Jesus from the law of sin and death.

That is, we have righteousness and life rather than sin and death before grace.

Now that we live in the time of grace, the time after Jesus died on the cross and rose from the dead. We live in a time of belief and righteousness and life through Jesus Christ, turning away from sin and death that was waiting for us behind the law.

We live 2,000 years out, more or less, from the time when Christ died and rose again. That's His first coming, His first advent. That means that we are 2,000 years closer to His second advent, and getting close to the rapture of the church. How do we know this? Look to Scripture. Look to Matthew 24, starting in verse 3:

> *As he sat on the Mount of Olives, the disciples came to him privately, saying, "Tell us, when will these things be, and what will be the sign of your coming and of the end of the age?"*

Well, that's a pretty straightforward question. Jesus gives him a pretty straightforward answer. Jesus said:

> *See that no one leads you astray. For many will come in my name, saying, 'I am the Christ,' and they will lead many astray. And you will hear of wars and rumors of wars. See that you are not alarmed, for this must take place, but the end is not yet. For nation will rise against nation, and kingdom against kingdom, and there will be famines and earthquakes in various places. All*

THE TIMES

these are but the beginning of the birth pains. Then they will deliver you up to tribulation and put you to death, and you will be hated by all nations for my name's sake. And then many will fall away and betray one another and hate one another. And many false prophets will arise and lead many astray. And because lawlessness will be increased, the love of many will grow cold. But the one who endures to the end will be saved. And this gospel of the kingdom will be proclaimed throughout the whole world as a testimony to all nations, and then the end will come. (Matthew 24:4b-14)

Jesus gives us the signs of the times. And the first one right here is that there will be a great deception among Christian people. Many will follow a false Christ. There will be churches that don't believe the Bible is the word of God. Churches will not preach that the blood of Jesus Christ is all that is necessary for the cleansing of your sin. Great deception amongst Christians will be a sign of the times, right before Jesus comes back.

Has you ever heard of Scientology? It's a big one these days; that's a false prophet that deceives many. Then you have Wicca, which flourishes in this county we live in. They don't do it out in the open, but it's there. They worship the devil right here amongst us. The Nation of Islam and Christian Science have got mosques and reading rooms in every big city.

False prophets shall arise and deceive many. And if you don't think that they're right here, amongst us, then you're wrong. Some of the most popular, some of the most heard,

THE TIMES

some of the people who have the biggest pulpits, are the biggest false Christs.

*And because lawlessness will be increased, the
love of many will grow cold.*

The love of many shall grow cold, even for Christians. Some churches will become churches full of people who won't reach out and help anybody because they're comfortable and happy right where they are. No one cares about anyone else.

You know what people care more about than caring for other people? They care more about seeing other people's distress than they do about caring for other people's needs. Turn on the afternoon television and watch some Jerry Springer for a while, and watch how people love to see other people in trouble or distress, not doing anything to help them but promoting the dysfunction and making the mockery of God.

If you don't have any love in your heart, when you see that kind of stuff going on, if your heart doesn't break, you got to get on your knees before Almighty God and ask Him to forgive you.

*And this gospel of the kingdom will be
proclaimed throughout the whole world as a
testimony to all nations, and then
the end will come.*

Radio, TV, missionaries; there's more gospel preaching going on right now in this world than there ever has been in the past. The Gideons are printing the Bible in 180 different countries in over 110 languages. Samaritan's Purse is reaching out into these places where people don't know Christ and preaching the gospel and giving them food and telling them about Jesus.

> ***This is the way the church needs to be working. We don't need false Christs and to lose our love for others. We need to increase our efforts, knowing that any day now, the rapture is coming.***

CHAPTER 55

Rapture

You can be that person that God says you can be if you just have some faith and move with Him. He took me, a drug addict, and put me in the pulpit. People are so quick to judge and care what other people think of them.

I care much more what God thinks about me that anyone else; and that's the mindset that you need to have also.

Quit caring what other people think and start caring about what God thinks. You'll see the power of God come into your life. You'll see lives change all around you.

I'm doing my very best to hasten the return of Jesus Christ. I will preach this gospel every time somebody calls me up. It is time to stop taking advantage of God's grace. That's what time it is.

This time of grace will end with the rapture of the church. Rapture – that's a taking away. You won't find that word in the Scripture, "rapture". But that's what it means. It means taking away.

Let's look at 1 Thessalonians 4:16-17:

For the Lord himself will descend from heaven with a cry of command, with the voice of an archangel, and with the sound of the trumpet of God. And the dead in Christ will rise first. Then we who are alive, who are left, will be caught up together with them in the clouds to meet the

RAPTURE

Lord in the air, and so we will always be with the Lord.

It is not a secret rapture either. Note that Paul said this event is announced with three incredible warning sounds:

For the Lord himself will descend from heaven with a <u>cry of command</u>, <u>with the voice of an archangel</u>, and with <u>the sound of the trumpet of God</u>.

We live in a time now where things are tough, but the grace of God flows.

It's time to stop taking advantage of the grace of God and begin to look up to heaven.

Remember that the Lord will be in the sky soon and take us to be with Him, amen.

There is a consequence for sin and there is a judgment to come. Flee the judgment, flee to Jesus; He's your only hope.

In Matthew 24:36, Jesus talks about this rapture. He's going show up. And He said:

But concerning that day and hour no one knows, not even the angels of heaven, nor the Son, but the Father only.

He's making a point here. No man knows that day or the hour, not even the angels know. Archangel Michael doesn't even know; only the Father knows.

Watch therefore, for you do not know what hour your Lord is coming.

RAPTURE

But know this, that if the master of the house had known in what part of the night the thief was coming, he would have stayed awake and would not have let his house be broken into. Therefore you also must be ready, for the Son of Man is coming at an hour you do not expect.
(Matthew 24:43)

    That's when He said He's coming; when you think He's not coming.

CHAPTER 56

Judgment of the Enemy

God will consign Satan and his demons to the Lake of Fire, according to Revelation 20:9-10:

And they marched up over the broad plain of the earth and surrounded the camp of the saints and the beloved city, but fire came down from heaven and consumed them [the nations opposed to God and His people], and the devil who had deceived them was thrown into the lake of fire and sulfur where the beast and the false prophet were, and they will be tormented day and night forever and ever.

You may ask, "Why all this suffering?"

Because Jesus is coming soon.

"Why all these problems? Why should I go after God? Why do I have all kinds of trouble?"

Because Jesus is coming soon.

Do you know what time it is? It's time to follow Jesus with faithfulness.

It is time to be different than the culture around us. It is time to live godly lives, resisting the influence of Satan and bringing glory to God!

CHAPTER 57

Hear the Word of God and Do It

God has not planned nor intended for us to grow stagnant in the Christian life.

There is always a new step to take in our pursuit with God, always a new level to attain, always new knowledge to be found, always a new truth to learn, always a new person to witness to, and always something more with God.

It is not God's intention for your faith to be weak or dull. He does not want your relationship with Him or the word of God to become dry, boring, and dull. That is the work of the enemy. God intends that you grow daily in your walk with Him.

We grow spiritually by growing in the grace and knowledge of God. Hear the word of God and do it.

How are you going to be blessed? Hear the word of God and obey it.

When Christians are not growing in Christ, they become stagnant. That means they are not bringing glory to Christ.

It also hurts the body of Christ when believers are crippled, broken and unproductive. Then you see a lot of people walking about professing to be Christians but having no demonstration of a change in their lives.

HEAR THE WORD OF GOD AND DO IT

This is the perfect time for you to choose to follow Jesus with faithfulness, seeking to obey His word, resist the enemy, and bring Him glory.

Salvation Prayer

Is there anything or anyone keeping you from accepting the FREE GIFT of eternal life found in Jesus Christ today? If you believe in the life, death, burial, and resurrection of Jesus, and if you are willing to believe with your heart, these five verses of truth, then the eternal life Jesus Christ promised will be yours.

We were all born into:

Sin—Romans 3:23 says:

> *For all have sinned and fall short*
> *of the glory of God. (NASB)*

Sin leads to **death**—Romans 6:23 says:

> *For the wages of sin is death, but the free gift of*
> *God is eternal life in Christ Jesus our Lord.*
> *(NASB)*

But it is God's **love** that was demonstrated in the atonement when Jesus Christ was willing to die in our place as a sacrifice for our sin, thus washing away the sin and death from your life.

Romans 5:8 says:

> *But God demonstrates His own love toward us,*
> *in that while we were yet sinners,*
> *Christ died for us. (NASB)*

Although God's love and forgiveness in Christ cannot be earned, most people reject Christ, thinking that they are good enough as they are to be accepted by God. So, since God's

SALVATION PRAYER

salvation cannot be earned, so how do you receive God's love and forgiveness?

By **faith**—Ephesians 2:8-9 says:

> *For by grace you have been saved,*
> *through faith; and not of yourselves,*
> *it is the [free] gift of God;*
> *not as a result of works,*
> *so that no one may boast. (NASB)*

There's nothing you can do to earn salvation. Rather, you have to place your trust in Jesus Christ and what He accomplished on the cross for you, then you can have **life.** Romans 10:9-10 says:

> *If you confess with your mouth Jesus as Lord,*
> *and believe in your heart that God raised Him*
> *from the dead, you will be saved; for with the*
> *heart a person believes, resulting in*
> *righteousness, and with the mouth he confesses,*
> *resulting in salvation. (NASB)*

Tell God that you trust His promise about the free gift of forgiveness for the sins in your life. Thank Him for sending His Son Jesus Christ to come and pay a debt that He didn't owe so that you could spend eternity with Him in heaven. If you need a little more direction, you can say a prayer like this:

> Lord, I know that I'm a sinner, but I thank You for Your Son, Jesus Christ, who died on the cross for my sins and rose on the third day so that I could be forgiven and spend eternity with You in heaven. I now freely accept Your sacrifice and trust You to direct me, to help me along the way of life, and to

SALVATION PRAYER

help me know You better. Thank You. In Jesus' name, I pray. Amen.

If you truly meant what you just prayed, the Bible says in 2 Corinthians 5:17 that you are now a **new creature**:

> *Therefore, if anyone is in Christ, he is a new creature; the old things have passed away; behold, new things have come. (NASB)*

From now on, you may feel different, or you may not. Emotions often follow and indicate a change of heart. However, it is God's word and the Holy Spirit that gives the assurance that you belong to Him (Romans 8:16).

The most important thing is that your sins have now been forgiven through faith in Jesus Christ and all that He has done. You now have the FREE gift of salvation and eternal life with Him. You have been set free from the "old things" (sin) to live a new life in Christ. You now have a new heart and a new Spirit living within you (Ezekiel 36:26-27). This may be a little hard to comprehend right now, but with time and understanding it will become clearer.

Know that henceforth you are not alone. You now have the Holy Spirit to comfort you (Acts 9:31), help you (Romans 8:26), teach you (Luke 2:12), guide you (John 16:13), and to give you spiritual gifts (1 Corinthians 12).

God loves you and desires to lead your life as you seek to follow Him daily. A new disciple of Christ abandons their "old" life to embrace a "new" life with Him. We are commanded in 2 Peter 3: 18 **to grow:**

> *But grow in the grace and knowledge of our Lord and Savior Jesus Christ. To Him be the*

SALVATION PRAYER

glory, both now and to the day of eternity.
Amen.

This is done through community, the church (Hebrews 10:25), through baptism (Matthew 28:19-20), through studying the Bible (Joshua 1:8), and prayer (Luke 18:1).

After this, we are told **to go** and share with others what it means to be a disciple of Christ:

And Jesus came up and spoke to them, saying, "All authority in heaven and on earth has been given to Me. Go, therefore, and make disciples of all the nations, baptizing them in the name of the Father and the Son and the Holy Spirit, teaching them to follow all that I commanded you; and behold, I am with you always, to the end of the age." (Matthew 28:18-20 NASB)

Tell others what God has done for you, how you have repented of your sins, and are now forgiven because of Jesus' sacrifice on the cross. Tell them how Jesus died for your sin, and rose again so that you could have a new life in Him. Tell others in love not only in words, but also deeds (Matthew 5:13-16). That's how you make disciples.

I'd like to thank Dr. Kyle Lance Martin and Time to Revive for these salvation notes, which were modified and used with permission.

If you enjoyed this read, you can find this and many of my other books available on Amazon.com

》》》 《《《

1. *Breaking God Into Prison: How to Successfully Transition From Incarceration Back Into Society*
2. *I Thought I Was Tough... Then I Went to Prison*
3. *Christian Leadership: And The Importance of Goals*
4. *2020 Vision: Clarity for Living Your Best Year Ever*
5. *Removing The Blinders: The Previously Untold Effects of The Original Sin on Mankind*
6. *Toxicity: Avoid It; Eliminate It*
7. *Breaking The Criminal Cycle Through Work*
8. *Discovering You*
9. *The Power of Christ in You*
10. *Just Going Through the Motions*
11. *Influencing Others*
12. *The Do's and Don'ts of Prison*
13. *How to Release Your Holy Ghost Power*
14. *From Your Heart To Your Head -Relationships*
15. *Prison Can't Hold You*
16. *18 Years Without Joy–(Fiction)*
17. *Judgments*
18. *Science Doesn't Refute the Bible, But Rather Confirms It*

19. *It's Never Too Late–(Fiction)*
20. *Interfering Idols*
21. *The Unrepentant Thief–(Fiction)*
22. *The Calendar Changed Have You?*
23. *A Felony Is Not The End*
24. *Build and Battle*
25. *Guided Prison Time*
26. *Stumbling Blocks to Stepping Stones*
27. *Dreams That Never Die*
28. *Unmasked: Seeing the Unfiltered Truth*
29. *Changed? Are You Really? Learning to Shine*
30. *The Angel House–(Fiction)*
31. *God, Are You There, Because I Can't Hear You*
32. *Choices, Consequences and Regrets: The Story of Jonah*
33. *Half-heart or Whole-heart; What Kind of Disciple are You?*
34. *The Temple: It's Time to Invest in Yourself*
35. *From Victim to Victor: Being a Champion*
36. *Christians Aren't Exempt: Overcoming Life's Obstacles*
37. *The Best Dressed Christian: An Invitation to Peace Means Wearing Your Armor*

38. *Sowing and Reaping: You Can't Harvest What You Are Unwilling to Plant*
39. *Christian Leadership Study Guide*
40. *Reaching Forth*
41. *English 101*
42. *Direction Without Doubt Part 1*
43. *Direction Without Doubt Part 2*
44. *Direction Without Doubt Part 3*
45. *Direction Without Doubt Study Guide*
46. *Prosperity: According to God*
47. *The Anointing: You Need It*
48. *One Nation Under God*
49. *We are Better Together*
50. *Looking Straight Ahead*
51. *Crisis or Opportunity*
52. *The False Prophet: The Father, The Grant Book Series #1–(Fiction)*
53. *Beautiful Things: The Son, The Grant Book Series #2–(Fiction)*
54. *Deception: The Daughter, The Grant Book Series #3–(Fiction)*
55. *Bearing Fruit: The Mother, The Grant Book Series #4–(Fiction)*
56. *Jars of Clay*

57. Salt and Light
58. Dangerous Prayers
59. It's a Process
60. Divine Reset for Restoration
61. Christ Centered Christmas
62. Family Matters
63. Leaving a Leader
64. Soul Matters: A Guide to the Matters of God
65. Wealth, Wisdom, and Your Way of Life
66. Transforming Your Mind and Spirit
67. The Boundary Book
68. An Inside Job
69. How to End Well
70. A Million Little Choices
71. High Interest
72. What Are You Searching For?
73. Jesus, The Anti-Christ, and You
74. Make a Choice
75. In the Valley
76. Choice Selection
77. Good Reception
78. Your Identity in Christ
79. Why Christians Suffer
80. Basic Evangelism

81. *Evangelism Daily Devotional*
82. *Faith in The Gap*
83. *You Know Better*
84. *The Casual Christian*
85. *You're Hurting Me*
86. *Information Leads to Transformation*
87. *A True Disciple*
88. *He Is*
89. *Lessons Learned While Waiting*
90. *The Toolbox*
91. *Seven Churches*
92. *Get Up and Move Forward Get Up and Move Forward*
93. *Chosen People: The Church in the World*
94. *Lessons for Leaders*
95. *Lessons Learned in a Cemetery*
96. *Taken Away: God's Vineyard*
97. *The Pursuing Father, the Prodigal Son, and the Prideful Son*
98. *Our Father*
99. *Waiting on God*
100. *The Collective Words of Wisdom Sermon Series 1: Let Love Burn Bright:*
101. *Finding Your Lover*

102. *The Collective Words of Wisdom Sermon Series 2: Real Talk*
103. *Make a U-Turn*
104. *Choose Wisdom*
105. *Christian Family*
106. *Peter*
107. *Velvet Mary*
108. *Defining Moments*
109. *Jesus and His*
110. *A Tale From The Trail (Fiction)*
111. *His Story, Your Story*
112. *America is Doomed*
113. *The Character of God*
114. *The Wonderful Spirit of God*
115. *The Christian Journey*
116. *Relating to the Holy Spirit*
117. *See My Servant*
118. *Overcoming the Evil One*
119. *How to Overcome*